D1384369

FOOD AS FOE

Nutrition and Eating Disorders

FOOD AS FOE

Nutrition and Eating Disorders

LESLI J. FAVOR

mc Marshall Cavendish
Benchmark
New York

Benchmark Books
Marshall Cavendish
99 White Plains Road
Tarrytown, NY 10591-9001
www.marshallcavendish.us
Text copyright © 2008 by Marshall Cavendish Corporation
Illustrations © 2008 by Marshall Cavendish Corporation

Library of Congress Cataloging-in-Publication Data
Favor, Lesli J.
Food as foe : nutrition and eating disorders / by Lesli J. Favor.
    p. cm.
Summary: "Provides a basic, comprehensive introduction to eating disorders, including
anorexia, bulimia, and binge eating, with a review of where to find help and how to make
wise food choices to become healthy"—Provided by publisher.
Includes bibliographical references and index.
ISBN-13: 978-0-7614-2553-3
1. Eating disorders. 2. Nutrition. I. Title.

RC552.E18F38 2007
616.85'26—dc22

2006101931

Digestive system illustration by Ian Warpole
Photo credits: Cover photo by Joyce Hesselberth/Images.com/CORBIS
PhotoEdit: David Kelly Crow, 8; Richard Hutchings, 28; Michael Newman, 46. *Corbis:* Phillip
Kaake, 16; Jack Hollingsworth, 24; David Raymer, 38; SGO/Image Point FR, 44; Tom
Stewart, 60; Nancy Ney, 88. *Getty Images:* Image Bank/ Yellow Dog Production, 20; Dave
Bennett, 49; Photonica, 36, 54; Bruce Aryes, 79; Tony Latham, 82; Odd Anderson/AFP, 94.
The Image Works: Topham, 62; Arlene Collins, 72.

Editor: Deborah Grahame
Publisher: Michelle Bisson
Art Director: Anahid Hamparian
Series Design: Becky Terhune

Charts in the appendixes are reprinted with permission from Dietary Reference Intakes for
Energy, Carbohydrate, Fiber, Fat, Fatty Acids, Cholesterol, Protein, and Amino Acids
(Macronutrients) © 2005 by the National Academy of Sciences, Courtesy of the National
Academies Press, Washington, D.C.

Printed in Malaysia
3 5 6 4

CONTENTS

INTRODUCTION

Selena *slumps on the floor of her friend's bathroom, retching into the toilet. She hopes the music from Eva's radio is loud enough to cover the sounds of her vomiting. None of the girls at Eva's sleepover know that Selena purges after indulging in food like the pizza they shared. Nor do they know that Selena makes up for eating in public by starving herself at home, sometimes surviving an entire weekend on two carrots and one celery stalk a day, plus all the diet soda she can drink. Serena feels tired all the time. On some days, it takes all of her concentration just to perform basic tasks.*

Selena has an eating disorder. Though she may feel painfully isolated in her situation, she is far from alone. Millions of Americans suffer from eating disorders such as anorexia, bulimia, and binge eating disorder. Experts estimate that between five and ten million Americans are affected by some eating disorder. Of teenage Americans, approximately one in every hundred is affected.

Joshua grimaces as he completes the twelfth repetition with the heavy barbell. After his upper body workout, he will start on his lower body. Dinner can wait. In fact, he will skip dinner altogether. If he can just add another inch to his pectorals and lose another inch from his waist . . . Joshua is already working out seven days a week, but he mentally pencils in two more workouts on weekends. Besides that, he will cut out another hundred calories a day. He tells himself that the hunger pangs are evidence that he is losing a little more body fat each day and making his muscles stand out that much more.

Joshua's case is similar to that of many males who suffer an eating disorder. They are torn between dueling desires to bulk up their muscles and to whittle away all traces of body fat. In response to these urges, their behaviors become extreme. Though fewer males than females suffer from eating disorders, the number of male sufferers is growing—and is expected to continue growing.

What is an eating disorder, exactly? The information in this book answers that question in detail. Psychiatrists Christopher G. Fairburn and B. Timothy Walsh, specialists in eating disorders, offer this succinct definition:

> An eating disorder is "a persistent disturbance of eating behavior or behavior intended to control weight, which significantly impairs physical health or psychosocial functioning. This disturbance should not be secondary to any recognized general medical disorder (e.g., a hypothalamic tumor) or any other psychiatric disorder (e.g., an anxiety disorder)."[1]

Someone with an eating disorder may severely restrict food intake, consume large amounts of food and then purge it from the body, exercise compulsively, or regularly eat huge amounts of food. The person's nutritional intake is compromised, and health risks for minor illnesses and major diseases increase. In some cases, death results.

This book offers information necessary to help you understand eating disorders, their risks, and treatment options. Nutrition is key to both the prevention and treatment of eating disorders. Consequently, chapters one, two, and three focus on food and patterns of eating, helping you to recognize healthy and unhealthy responses to food. The three main eating disorders— anorexia, bulimia, and binge eating disorder—are the subjects of chapters seven, eight, and nine, while the final chapter examines additional eating disorders. Throughout, we will examine aspects of ordered and disordered eating, including related issues of self-image, body weight, and mental wellness.

Eating disorders are serious health threats, but with information and understanding, you are better equipped to recognize early symptoms and prevent eating disorders from occurring. Young people who already suffer from an eating disorder are better informed about how—and why—to get crucial professional help.

Consuming food nourishes the body, but choosing to eat or not to eat sometimes is a way of expressing emotions that are too difficult to put into words.

Myth: A thin person is a healthy person.
Fact: A thin person with poor eating and exercise habits can be just as unhealthy as an overweight person with poor eating and exercise habits.

1
FOOD: FRIEND OR FOE?

We eat to stay alive. It's that simple—or is it? On one hand, as children we are taught that food makes us healthy and helps us grow big and strong. On the other hand, as we get older and make our own food choices, we learn that some foods are more healthful than others and that a variety of foods as well as portion sizes are essential to good health. In addition, without realizing it, we eat for reasons other than simply to stay alive and healthy. We eat to fuel—or fight—emotions, and we eat because those around us are eating. We also eat—or refuse to eat—in response to messages and images from the media, our family and social group, and in response to our own body image.

In short, eating is no simple matter. It can involve serious psychological and physical issues. In fact, an estimated five to ten million Americans have some type of eating disorder that disturbs their normal physical and/or mental health.[1]

In light of this complexity, food—simple and life sustaining though it may be—becomes charged with conflicting desires, confusion, and controversy. Sure, food is a friend, keeping us alive and enabling our bodies to function. But when eating habits become entangled with emotions, peer influences, differing media messages, or poor body image, food can easily become a foe.

What does all this mean to you? Taking a close look at why you eat can help you understand the roles food plays in your own life, whether healthy or unhealthy. This can help you to understand why you eat or choose not to eat and is a starting point for your examining the roles food and nutrition play in your daily life.

FOOD AND PHYSICAL GROWTH

For young people, nutritious food is critical to physical growth during puberty and adolescence. In this time a young person's body grows and develops rapidly. During this period, called the growth spurt, which typically unfolds over two to three years, girls commonly grow around three inches taller and gain from ten to thirty pounds. A boy's growth spurt may add eight inches or more in height with a corresponding gain in weight—perhaps ten pounds or more in just a year.

At this time of heightened nutritional need, many young people begin to take charge of their own food choices and eating habits. Ironically, they may know little, if anything, about the foods and serving sizes that must nourish their bodies while going through this crucial development phase.

At the same time, young people become increasingly aware of their own bodies. They and their friends share opinions about body shapes and sizes, and in private they grapple with their own body image. They may wonder if they are too short, too tall, too fat, too thin. Attitudes toward food and its effect on the body take shape, and a young person may make food choices aimed at achieving a specific body shape or size, ignoring the diet's possible ill effects.

This combination of rapid physical growth, increased

personal independence, developing body image, and other life situations produces a stressful environment. Attempting to cope, some young people develop an eating disorder, an illness that causes a person to practice a harmful pattern of eating. Examples include not eating enough, binging and then purging food (such as by induced vomiting), and excessive dieting and exercising. The most common eating disorders are anorexia nervosa, bulimia nervosa, and binge eating disorder.

FOOD AND EMOTIONS

It is easy to see how food becomes entangled with our emotions. In infancy our needs are quite basic, with nourishment ranking high on the list. Feeding an infant provides consistent physical sustenance as well as emotional nourishment through being carried, cuddled, and touched. An infant gains a great deal of well-being through eating rituals.

As children grow older, the tastes, textures, and smells of certain foods become associated with particular emotions. Arriving home to the smell of baking chicken may evoke a sense of contentment—dinner's almost ready, all is well. The smell of cookies from a grandparent's kitchen may make us feel loved. Hot soup on a winter's day may make us feel snug, and a picnic with grilled hamburgers may make us feel festive and carefree. By the time we leave childhood, most of us have "comfort foods" that evoke a sense of security, reminding us of when we ate those foods as children.

Some foods, however, become associated with either rewards or punishments. *Did you eat all your dinner? You deserve a slice of chocolate cake! You didn't finish your broccoli? No apple pie for you tonight! Did you make straight A's on your report card? We'll celebrate with pepperoni pizza!* Some caregivers use food as emotional manipulation, further cementing the bond between food and feelings. *If you behave during the movie, you'll get hot dogs afterward. If you act up at the table, you'll sit there until you eat every bite.*

We also associate certain foods with holidays or family celebrations. At Thanksgiving, eating turkey, dressing, and green-bean casserole with our extended family may give us a warm sense of belonging. A box of chocolates from a sweetheart on Valentine's Day can inspire romantic feelings. A Latino family may ring in the new year with a meal of homemade tamales or pasteles, while a Chinese family may celebrate the new year by eating lo han jai, a vegetable stew. These traditions of eating evoke an awareness of our place within our familial and cultural heritage. As a result, food holds a powerful place in our lives.

In addition, some foods are proven to influence our emotions and energy levels. Chocolate, for instance, triggers the brain's release of opioids, chemicals that make us feel good by increasing our sense of contentment. Caffeine and sugar provide quick bursts of energy. Consequently some people cannot face the morning without their cup of coffee, strong tea, or caffeinated soda.

Is it any wonder that food and emotions become tightly linked? For a person struggling to establish healthy eating behaviors or coping with an eating disorder, emotions can make it much harder to achieve a solid nutritional diet.

FOOD AND SOCIAL SETTINGS

Food gains significance in our lives through its association with social activities and settings. Religious ceremonies or traditions, for instance, link certain foods to a person's sense of religious identity. During Passover, Jews eat unleavened (flat, like crackers) bread called matzo, and they eat foods including cabbage, dates, apples, and honey, each symbolizing something special, during Rosh Hashanah. Many Christians observe Easter with a special meal, often including baked ham. Children decorate Easter eggs and may be given an Easter basket containing chocolates and other sweets.

Religious restrictions on eating and on certain foods, however, are very common, either during specific times or as a matter of course. Muslims prohibit foods containing pork (as do Jews) or gelatin and breads made with dried yeast. Muslims also observe the month of Ramadan by fasting during daylight hours. Some followers of the Hindu religion do not eat meat, and many Catholics do not eat meat on Fridays during Lent. In situations such as these, food attains significance—even power—through the practice of abstinence, not indulgence.

Besides religious practices, many family traditions celebrate food. These customs, too, help bond specific foods to feelings of love, security, happiness, and well-being. Birthday cakes, Sunday morning pancakes, Dad's grilled burgers, Mom's famous meat loaf, and Friday night pizza are typical examples. Foods that evoke an emotional response tend to take on increased importance in a person's eating habits. Instead of following a nutritionally sound diet, people may allow emotions to govern what they eat.

When it comes to food choices, young people are particularly vulnerable to peer influences. A teenage girl may eat nothing but a green-lettuce salad for lunch, even though she will become hungry later, because that is what her friends are eating. A slim boy who hopes to make the football team may routinely overload his plate with carbohydrates and protein-dense foods to "bulk up." An overweight teen may eat moderately while around his friends but then ravenously devour huge portions when alone. Few young people are completely free of food-related pressures from peers, whether or not these pressures are imposed intentionally.

FOOD AND THE MEDIA

By celebrating ultrathin female celebrities and overmuscled sexy males, the media does little to encourage a healthy attitude toward food. Magazines and celebrity-gossip television shows obsessively track prominent actresses' fluctuations in weight. One week they praise them as stunning and the next week judge them as being dangerously thin. Primetime television and movies often feature thin, even scrawny, actresses in leading roles. Male starring roles idealize images of muscled, fat-free bodies. Articles and interviews about upcoming films commonly include accounts of how an actress or actor lost (or, rarely, gained) weight to prepare for a role.

The body of an average person stands in stark contrast to the bodies of those who make a living by, among other things, being thin. According to the National Center for Health Statistics, the weight of sixteen-year-old boys was about 164 pounds in 2002, with an average height of 5 feet 9 inches. Weight of girls of the same age was about 139 pounds and height just under 5 feet 4 inches. The average male in his thirties was 189 pounds and 5 feet 9.5 inches tall. The average female in her thirties was 163 pounds and just over 5 feet 4 inches tall.[2] What do these numbers suggest? That an average person who eats a nutritious diet may find it difficult or impossible to achieve a model-thin body.

FOOD AND BODY IMAGE

We develop a perception of our appearance—our body image—in response to many factors, including how we feel "in our own skin," how we think others see us, and how we think we measure up to the physical standards of friends, family, or the media. Ultimately these thoughts link to food, for it is with food that we fuel our quest for a good body image or tinker with our nutrition in reaction to a poor one.

A poor body image frequently coincides with an eating disorder. For example, a girl may feel overweight when, in fact, she is at or below normal weight. She becomes preoccupied with being thin and develops a fear of gaining weight. She eats less and less. She equates food with feeling fat and becomes disgusted with food. This scenario is typical of many who suffer from anorexia.

Those who suffer from bulimia have similar perceptions of their bodies. They place a high value on body weight or body size, striving to weigh less or to be thinner. Though they often have a normal weight, their distorted body image drives them to purge themselves of food or to exercise compulsively.

Realizing how emotions can influence your daily food choices is a key step in learning good food habits and maintaining a realistic self-image. Understanding healthy and unhealthy patterns of eating—the subject of the next chapter—is equally important.

It's not easy figuring out which foods to eat, and in what amounts, to form a diet that is both nutritious and enjoyable.

Myth: *Potatoes and bread make you fat.*
Fact: *Gram for gram, potatoes and bread provide the same number of calories as protein and less than half the calories of fat.*

2
HEALTHY AND UNHEALTHY PATTERNS OF EATING

When it comes to establishing healthy eating behaviors, food and nutrition can seem like hazardous fields of land mines. Each day involves a series of food choices—when, what, and how much to eat. These choices can easily become overwhelming. It's certainly easier to simply eat whatever is most convenient or appealing. It's when you are consciously trying to follow a beneficial eating pattern that you need helpful road signs guiding you toward that goal.

You may be surprised to know that healthy patterns of eating vary widely. There is no single right way to structure daily meals and snacks. A teenager in good shape may eat three home-cooked meals one day, taking in a balance of the three major nutrients: proteins, carbohydrates, and fats. The next day the same teen may have cold cheese pizza for breakfast, a fruit smoothie for lunch, and fast food for dinner, or eat two, four, or even five mini-meals. Such variations in eating practices are normal and can be part of eating that is good for you. Recognizing healthy and unhealthy patterns of eating over time is more important than just sticking to a regimented meal and snack system.

An adult who follows a pattern of eating healthfully when

hungry, ceasing to eat when full, and exercising moderately tends to maintain a steady weight. This weight, called the body's set point, may fluctuate five to ten pounds. However, as long as the pattern of eating and exercising stays consistent, the weight range stays consistent. On one hand, eating for emotional comfort instead of in response to hunger, for instance, can push the body's weight above the set point. On the other hand, a child or teenager, whose body is still growing, will not establish a set point for weight until the body's growth is complete.

HEALTHY EATING

As discussed in chapter one, we eat for many reasons, including emotions, social settings, media messages, and body image. At the most basic level, we eat to fuel our bodies. Hunger drives us to eat, and feeling satisfied or full (called satiety) cues us to stop eating. Our bodies use the energy gained from food to carry out essential functions such as breathing, pumping blood, and growing new cells.

A nourishing pattern of eating, or a healthy diet, creates a balance between the intake of energy through food and the expenditure of energy by bodily functions. To measure the energy in food, we use the kilocalorie, commonly called the calorie. Scientifically, 1 calorie is the quantity of heat energy required to raise the temperature of 1 gram of water by 1 degree Celsius at 1 atmospheric pressure. You don't have to be a scientist, though, to understand the role of calories in a healthy diet. You just want to eat the number of calories your body needs to carry out its normal processes, including growth and development. Additionally, those calories should come from a nutritious selection of foods rather than so-called fast or junk foods.

The calorie content of each type of nutrient varies. Fat

provides the most calories, 9 calories per gram, while carbohydrates and proteins each provide 4 calories per gram. Eating too many calories results in the storage of excess calories as body fat. Conversely, eating too few calories interferes with the body's functions and can disrupt normal growth and development.

To get an idea of how many calories you need per day, examine the chart "Recommended daily calorie Intake." It shows a moderately active person's need for calories as he or she gets older. Depending on your height and level of physical activity, you may need more or fewer calories than the amount shown. An athlete, for example, needs more calories during times of training and competition.

Recommended daily calorie intake for a moderately active individual

GENDER	AGE (IN YEARS)	DAILY CALORIE INTAKE
Child	2—3	1,000—1,400
Female	4—8	1,400—1,600
	9—13	1,600—2,000
	14—18	2,000
	19—30	2,000—2,200
	31—50	2,000
	51+	1,800
Male	4—8	1,400—1,600
	9—13	1,800—2,200
	14—18	2,400—2,800
	19—30	2,600—2,800
	31—50	2,400—2,600
	51+	2,200—2,400

Source: Adapted from United States Department of Health and Human Services, United States Department of Agriculture, *Dietary Guidelines for Americans 2005.*

Though calories are important, the calorie is not the only measuring stick for wholesome eating. A regular pattern of daily meals and snacks that together achieve the proper balance of nutritious foods completes the plan. There are six classes of nutrients: carbohydrates, proteins, lipids (fats), vitamins, minerals, and water. To remain healthy, your body needs particular amounts of these nutrients on a regular basis. Different tools are available to help you plan meals and snacks to attain this balance. Such aids include charts of recommended dietary reference intakes (DRIs) of nutrients and the food guide pyramid. These are examined in chapter three, along with a closer look at each class of nutrient.

The physiological drive of hunger is a good indicator of when to eat. It is your body's way of saying it needs energy. Due to daily schedules and routines such as school, work, and other responsibilities, however, you may not be able to eat at

A nutritious lunch fuels your body for the afternoon's demands on your mental and physical energy.

Caffeine is a stimulant that affects the central nervous system, raising the heart rate. After drinking a caffeinated soda or coffee, for example, you likely will feel a boost of energy and alertness. Large amounts of caffeine, however, can cause jitteriness, dizziness, anxiety, or headaches.

Since caffeine supplies temporary bursts of energy, people trying to reduce their calorie intake may drink caffeinated diet sodas instead of eating food. This practice has been linked both to dieters and to people with eating disorders such as anorexia. Replacing food with caffeine, however, is not good for the body. Besides the loss of nutrients from food not eaten, there are other negative consequences:

• **Caffeine builds dependency.** Over time, the more caffeine a person consumes, the more of it he or she needs to get the same boost in energy or alertness. This is known as tolerance.

• **Caffeine is addictive.** When people who habitually consume caffeine reduce or eliminate the drug, they experience withdrawal symptoms such as headaches, muscle aches, depression, and irritability.

• **Caffeine dehydrates the body.** The drug causes an increased need to urinate that, in large volume, can cause a loss of such necessary minerals as calcium and potassium.

In a balanced diet, caffeine is limited to an occasional treat. See the chart *The Amount of Caffeine in Common Drinks and Snacks.*

The Amount of Caffeine in Common Drinks and Snacks

DRINK/SNACK	AMOUNT OF DRINK/SNACK	AMOUNT OF CAFFEINE
Brewed coffee	8 ounces	65–120 mg
Iced tea	8 ounces	9–50 mg
Mountain Dew	12 ounces	55 mg
Diet Coke	12 ounces	45 mg
Pepsi	12 ounces	38 mg
Hershey's Special Dark chocolate bar	1.45 ounces	31 mg
Hershey's chocolate bar	1.55 ounces	10 mg

the exact times you are hungry. So do take advantage of scheduled lunch or snack breaks, which offer opportunities to eat responsively to your body's normal needs.

Eating on a regular schedule can, in fact, condition your body to expect food around the same times each day. For instance, while you may not actually feel hungry during your assigned lunch break, you are likely to have a desire to eat anyway, because "it's time to eat." You may know from experience that if you don't eat during that break, hunger pangs will soon plague you. Balancing schedule with your body's natural appetite is part of setting up a pattern of healthy eating.

UNHEALTHY EATING

Many types of unhealthy eating behaviors exist, but they all exhibit one thing—lack of balance. While a healthy diet achieves a balance of nutrients and calories according to the individual's needs, an unhealthy diet is skewed to one extreme or the other. An obese individual, for example, typically consumes more calories than necessary, while an anorexic consumes too few calories or nutrients. Still, an explanation of unhealthy eating is not as simple as merely overeating or undereating.

Going back to the discussion in chapter one, various factors influence a person's attitude toward food. Placing too much emotional importance on food or having a negative body image can lead to unhealthy eating behaviors. Eating disorders develop when a person's relationship with food fails to center on nutritional balance. Instead, it zeroes in on some harmful factor, such as emotional discomfort or repulsion by the feel of food in the mouth or stomach. Warning signs of an eating disorder include the following.

Food behaviors: regularly skipping meals or eating only tiny amounts, making regular excuses for not eating, limiting foods to low-calorie choices such as lettuce and celery, hiding or disposing of food supposedly eaten.

Body image behaviors: insisting that she/he is fat when this is not true, expressing disgust or contempt for body size or shape, wearing clothing to conceal an emaciated body, purging food by using laxatives, diuretics, or other aids.

Exercise behaviors: compulsively exercising, often to the point of exhaustion, and frequently in combination with severely restricted food intake.

Thoughts and feelings: believing that being lean will bestow happiness, love, or some other emotional benefit; believing that thin people are happier or more successful than those with average bodies; denying—often angrily—that he or she has an eating problem; feeling envious of anyone who is thinner; feeling guilty, unworthy, hopeless, powerless, unloved, inadequate, or the like.[1]

It is worth keeping in mind that a person showing one or two warning signs of an eating disorder—especially if only temporarily—may not actually have a full-blown eating disorder. It is not uncommon, or even abnormal, for a person to feel doubts about his or her weight, size, or self-worth. These are ordinary to eating concerns. A true eating disorder is more serious in that the behaviors, thoughts, and feelings persist and worsen over time and the person's physical well-being and psychosocial health deteriorate.

Closer examinations of particular eating disorders follow in chapters four through ten. First, though, chapter three provides a base of knowledge about nutrition and wellness.

Sharing a meal with friends is socially as well as physically satisfying.

Myth: *Eating lots of protein makes your muscles get big.*
Fact: *Eating a balance of protein, carbohydrates, and fat combined with physical training results in muscle development. Eating too much protein causes the body to store the extra energy as fat.*

3
NUTRITION AND WELLNESS

Good nutrition contributes to your overall wellness, a combination of your physical and mental health. Poor nutrition, which becomes part of eating disorders, disintegrates not only your body's wellness but your psychosocial wellness, too.

The body is designed to thrive on healthful foods. In particular, the digestive process ensures that nutrients in foods and drinks are processed and used throughout the body. Knowing how the body processes food may help you understand your body's need for good nutrition. It may also help you recognize the damages caused by eating disorders.

The moment food or drink is put into the mouth, the body begins to extract nutrition. While food is chewed, glands in the mouth produce saliva that lubricates the food and begins to break down starches into smaller particles. When food is swallowed, it passes through the esophagus to the stomach, where food and liquid are mixed with digestive juices that further break down the food particles. Next, the partially digested matter empties into the small intestine, where fluids from the intestine, the pancreas, and the liver continue the process. Finally, the remaining molecules of food, along with water and minerals, are absorbed through the small and large intestinal walls. They are carried by the bloodstream throughout the body for storage or for further processing, depending on the nutrient. Waste matter (such as fiber and used cells

THE DIGESTIVE SYSTEM

Mouth and salivary glands

Esophagus

Liver

Gallbladder

Stomach

Pancreas

Duodenum

Transverse colon

Descending colon

Ascending colon

Jejunum

Cecum

Small Intestine

Ileum

Appendix

Sigmoid colon

Rectum

Anus

The complex digestive system breaks down food so that it is usable by the body.

shed from intestinal walls) is pushed into the colon and expelled as feces.

The digestive process breaks food into components that are used for energy, for body structures (bones, muscles, and body fat), and for the regulation of such body functions as controlling body temperature and chemical reactions. The body needs more than forty nutrients to stay alive and healthy. Nutrition, however, doesn't have to be complicated. Although many books and Web sites are available on the subject, you can plan your nutrition by grasping a few key concepts and using a daily eating guide such as the food guide pyramid. These topics are discussed in this chapter.

THE SIX CLASSES OF NUTRIENTS

The forty-plus nutrients the body needs to survive are grouped into six classes: carbohydrates, proteins, lipids (fats), vitamins, minerals, and water.

Carbohydrates

Carbohydrates include sugars, starches, and most fibers. Foods rich in carbohydrates include cereals, grains, vegetables, pasta, potatoes, and sugary foods and drinks. Most carbohydrates—the sugars and the starches—are converted by the body into glucose, an energy source for the body. While most fiber is not usable as energy, it is important to the health of the digestive tract. Fiber is found in whole grains, vegetables, fruits, and legumes (peas, beans, and lentils).

Carbohydrates occur in two forms: simple and complex. Simple carbohydrates include the naturally occurring sugar in fruit called fructose. Simple carbohydrates also include the sugars in syrups, honey, and sucrose, the white processed sugar used in baked goods and sweetened beverages. Simple carbohydrates are sources of quick energy because they are

Most foods contain a variety of nutrients, though foods often have a dominant class of nutrient that helps us categorize foods and plan meals.

easily converted to glucose and rapidly enter the bloodstream. Complex carbohydrates, found in most grain products, vegetables, and potatoes, are digested more slowly. They provide energy over a longer period of time.

Proteins

Protein is formed of chains of amino acids. The body uses these amino acid proteins for the growth and repair of tissues such as muscle, bone, cartilage, and teeth. Amino acids also help regulate bodily functions, such as carrying oxygen to cells and fighting infection. When carbohydrates are unavailable, proteins can be converted to glucose for energy. High-protein foods include eggs, milk, meat, fish, and poultry, as well as certain vegetables, grains, and beans.

Lipids

Lipids (fats) are present in foods derived both from animals and plants. Like carbohydrates, lipids are a good source

All fats provide 9 calories per gram, but all fats are not equally healthful. Here are several different kinds of fats that you will find in foods. The first one listed, monounsaturated fat, is considered the most healthful, while trans fat, listed last, is the least healthful.

Monounsaturated fat

This fat is a liquid at room temperature but may become cloudy or semisolid in the refrigerator. You'll find it in olive, canola, and nut oils as well as in avocados, almonds, cashews, and other nuts. This fat is considered good because it helps lower blood cholesterol.

Polyunsaturated fat

This fat is a liquid both at room temperature and in the refrigerator. You'll find it in vegetable oils, pecans, and cold-water fish, such as salmon. On one hand, this fat can help lower blood cholesterol levels. On the other hand, the process of lowering cholesterol can be limited by certain other chemical processes in the body.

Saturated fat

This fat is usually solid or waxy at room temperature. You'll find it in red meats, dairy products, and tropical oils, such as coconut and palm. This kind of fat can raise blood cholesterol levels and increase your risk of coronary artery disease.

Trans fat

This fat is sometimes called "partially hydrogenated vegetable oils." It is considered a bad fat because it raises blood cholesterol levels. You'll find it in shortening, most margarines, and food prepared with shortening and margarine, such as cookies and crackers.

Triglycerides are the main component of fats. When we talk about the fat content of a food, we are talking about triglycerides. Triglycerides are made up of three fatty acids and glycerol. Depending on how the fatty acids and glycerol are combined, the fat may be saturated or unsaturated. Saturated fats are solid at room temperature. Think of a stick of butter or the veins of fat in a raw steak. Unsaturated fats are liquid at room temperature. Unsaturated fats are found in cooking oils and nonliquid foods such as nuts, olives, and fish.

of energy. Moreover, the body needs fats for cell membrane structure, for blood-clotting functions, and to transport the fat-soluble vitamins A, D, E, and K throughout the body.

Vitamins

Vitamins are organic substances found in tiny amounts in plant and animal foods. Although vitamins do not provide energy, they are vital to the body's metabolic processes that yield energy. Additionally, the body uses certain vitamins to maintain the health of eyes and bones. Still other vitamins play roles in blood clotting and tissue growth and development. Antioxidants, such as vitamin E, protect against free radicals, by-products of oxidation in cells that can damage or destroy cells.

Some vitamins are water-soluble and others are fat-soluble. This means that some are carried within the body by water and some by fat. The B-complex vitamins and vitamin C are water-soluble, while vitamins A, D, E, and K are fat-soluble.

Minerals

In contrast to vitamins, which are organic substances, minerals are inorganic (they do not contain carbon). Plants obtain minerals from soil and water, animals obtain minerals by eating plants and drinking water, and humans obtain minerals by eating plants and animals. Like vitamins, minerals do not provide energy but are essential to life-sustaining bodily processes. Some minerals are vital to the structures of bones, teeth, and muscles. Others are necessary for enzymes to function, enabling chemical reactions in the body. Still others, called electrolytes, help balance fluids throughout the body and help regulate the acid-base content of the blood.

Reading the Nutrition Facts labels on foods and beverages helps you understand the specific nutrients you are consuming. The Food and Drug Administration (FDA) requires these labels on all regulated food products. A few exceptions include very tiny packages and fast food. To ensure reliability and accuracy of labeling nationwide, all food packagers must use the same format for the Nutrition Facts label. Each label lists information for one normal-sized serving of the food or drink. For example, a manufacturer cannot list an absurdly small serving size of a snack food to make it seem low calorie or to obscure its actual fat content.

See the sample label for a container of apricot-mango yogurt, at right.

The "% Daily Value" numbers (sometimes written %DV) help you judge how much of your daily needs are met by this product. For example, for a 2,000-calorie diet, the container of yogurt provides 25 percent of your calcium needs for the day—a significant amount. On the other hand, the yogurt provides only 6 percent of vitamin C for the day. Using this information, you could balance this snack by drinking a few ounces of citrus juice to get additional vitamin C.

Nutrition Facts

Serving Size 1 container (170g)
Servings Per Container 1

Amount Per Serving

Calories 160

Calories from Fat 15

	% Daily Values*
Total Fat 2g	3%
Saturated Fat 1g	5%
Trans Fat 0g	
Cholesterol 10mg	3%
Sodium 110mg	5%
Total Carbohydrate 30g	10%
Dietary Fiber 2g	8%
Sugars 29g	
Protein 7g	
Vitamin A	8%
Vitamin C	6%
Calcium	25%
Iron	4%

* Percent Daily Values are based on a 2,000-calorie diet. Your daily values may be higher or lower depending on your calorie needs.

Calories:		2,000	2,500
Total Fat	Less than	65g	80g
Sat Fat	Less than	20g	25g
Cholesterol	Less than	300mg	300mg
Sodium	Less than	2,400mg	2,400mg
Total Carbohydrate		300g	375g
Dietary Fiber		25g	30g

The Nutrition Facts labels on food packages provide information needed to fit a food or beverage into a healthy plan of eating.

DIETARY REFERENCE INTAKES
FOR TEENAGERS

	MALES AGES 14–19	FEMALES AGES 14–19
Total water (8-ounce cup)	14–15	10–11
Carbohydrate (gram)	130	130
Protein (gram)	52–56	46
Vitamin A (microgram)	625–630	485–500
Vitamin C (milligram)	63–75	56–60
Vitamin E (milligram)	12	12
Thiamin (milligram)	1.0	0.9
Riboflavin (milligram)	1.1	0.9
Niacin (milligram)	12	11
Vitamin B6 (milligram)	1.1	1.0-1.1
Folate (microgram)	320–330	320–330
Vitamin B12 (microgram)	2.0	2.0
Copper (microgram)	685–700	685–700
Iodine (microgram)	95	95
Iron (milligram)	6.0–7.7	7.9–8.1
Magnesium (milligram)	330–340	255–300
Molybdenum (microgram)	33–34	33–34
Phosphorus (milligram)	1,055 (ages 14–18)	1,055 (ages 14–18)
	580 (age 19)	580 (age 19)
Selenium (microgram)	45	45
Zinc (milligram)	8.5–9.4	6.8–7.3

* Total water includes all water consumed through food, beverages, and drinking water. Source: Adapted from Food and Nutrition Board, The National Academy of Sciences.

Water

An adult's body is made up of 50 to 65 percent water. An infant's body is about 70 to 85 percent water. Without taking in water, the human body can survive only a few days. For one thing, nearly every chemical reaction within the body uses water. Water is also crucial to digestion, to the absorption and transportation of nutrients, to the growth and repair of tissues, and to the removal of waste through urination. Water also helps regulate body temperature and maintain body structure. To include water in your diet, you can drink plain water or water mixed into other beverages, or eat solid foods containing water, such as fruits and vegetables.

A NUTRITIOUS DIET

The body needs nutrients in varying amounts. For example, proteins and carbohydrates are needed in greater amounts than vitamins and minerals. A nutritious diet includes the balance of nutrients right for your body, taking into account your gender, age, level of physical activity, and other factors such as illness or pregnancy.

To determine the amounts of nutrients your body needs daily, you can consult the dietary reference intakes (DRIs) charts created by the Food and Nutrition Board of the National Academy of Sciences. In the back of this book, you will find the full charts, devised for people of all ages. The first chart included in this chapter shows DRIs for teenagers.

MY PYRAMID

The DRIs chart is useful for learning the amounts of individual nutrients that make up a healthy diet. On a daily basis, however, it is impractical to count the exact amounts of nutrients in each food you eat. To form a daily eating plan, you can use a guide that recommends numbers of servings of different food groups.

The United States Department of Agriculture developed a visual guide for daily eating called MyPyramid. As you can see in the illustration, MyPyramid uses bands of different colors to represent the five major food groups plus oils. A healthy diet includes foods from each group every day.

The bands on the pyramid are different widths to show the relative proportions of each food group. Notice that the widest band is grains. Your daily diet should include more grain products than any other foods. The bands for vegetables and milk are about the same size. Include each of these food groups in amounts slightly smaller than grains. Fruits and meat and beans are proportionately smaller, so include these foods in lesser amounts. The slimmest band is oils; include only a little oil in your daily diet. On the left side of the pyramid, the figure climbing steps is a reminder to stay physically active along with eating nutritiously.

RECOMMENDED DAILY FOOD INTAKES FOR TEENAGERS

Calorie level	2,000	2,200	2,400	2,600	2,800
Grains	6 oz.	7 oz.	8 oz.	9 oz.	10 oz.
Vegetables	2.5 cups	3 cups	3 cups	3.5 cups	3.5 cups
Fruits	2 cups	2 cups	2 cups	2 cups	2.5 cups
Oils	6 tsp.	6 tsp.	7 tsp.	8 tsp.	8 tsp.
Milk	3 cups	3 cups	3 cups	3 cups	3 cups
Meat and Beans	5.5 oz.	6 oz.	6.5 oz.	6.5 oz.	7 oz.
Discretionary calorie allowance*	267	290	362	410	426

* The discretionary calorie allowance is the number of calories left over after accounting for the foods listed in the column above it. The individual should choose additional foods, according to preference, to meet this allowance.
Source: Adapted from United States Department of Agriculture, "MyPyramid: Food Intake Patterns."

A METRIC CONVERSION CHART FOR MEASUREMENTS USED THROUGHOUT THIS BOOK IS FOUND ON PAGE 106.

Most teenagers need 2,000—2,800 calories a day to supply their energy needs. The chart "Recommended daily food intakes for teenagers" lists recommended daily amounts of each food group, plus oils/fats, to satisfy these energy needs.

In the food guide pyramid, the grains group includes foods made from wheat, rice, oats, cornmeal, and barley. In general a serving is one slice of bread, one cup of cold breakfast cereal, or a half-cup of cooked rice, pasta, or oatmeal.

The vegetables group includes both vegetables and vegetable juices. One serving from this group is, for example, one cup of raw or cooked vegetables, one cup of vegetable juice, or two cups of raw, leafy greens.

Fruit juice is naturally and healthfully sweet, making added sugars or sweeteners unnecessary.

The fruits group includes fruits and fruit juices. A serving is generally one cup of fruit or fruit juice or a half-cup of dried fruit.

The oils group includes butter and liquid oils, such as corn oil, canola oil, and olive oil, as well as the oils found in nuts, fish, avocados, mayonnaise, salad dressings, margarine, and other foods.

The milk group includes all milk and dairy products that retain their calcium content. For example, yogurt is part of the milk group, but butter—a milk product—is part of the oils group. A serving in this group is one cup of milk or yogurt, an ounce-and-a-half of natural cheese (such as cheddar or Swiss), or two ounces of processed cheese (such as Velveeta or American).

The meat and beans group contains a variety of protein-rich foods. A one-ounce serving in this group is the equivalent of one ounce of lean meat, poultry, or fish; a quarter-cup of dry beans, cooked; one egg; one tablespoon of peanut butter; or a half-ounce of nuts or seeds.

At first, using guides such as the DRIs and MyPyramid may take a little effort. Once you develop a sense of what kinds of foods and portions make up a healthy diet, however, you can create nutritious meals and snacks on your own. Learning how to meet your personal nutrition needs in this way boosts your overall sense of well-being. Your knowledge of basic nutrition not only helps you stay healthy, but it also helps you appreciate the harmful effects of eating disorders, which are discussed in the following chapters.

An eating disorder wreaks havoc not just on physical health, but on mental well-being and quality of life, too.

4
WHAT ARE EATING DISORDERS?

By the time young people become teenagers, many of them have heard of eating disorders. If pressed, they may have a vague idea that an eating disorder means eating too much or too little. They may think that anyone who is "too skinny" or "too fat" has an eating disorder. In some cases they may have heard a friend or fellow student called "that anorexic girl" or "the bulimic guy." Eating disorders, however, are not as simple as losing or gaining weight or being a picky eater.

It is not uncommon for children and adolescents to go through phases of eating in different ways, of experimenting with new food plans such as vegetarianism, or of expressing strong dietary likes and dislikes. A young person's weight fluctuates depending on many factors, including growth spurts and normal growth and development. The truth is, not every skinny person or overweight person has an eating problem.

So how does an eating disorder differ from "normal" concerns about body size and weight? An eating disorder becomes entrenched as habit. It is not temporary, and it involves severe health and psychological problems. It is an illness, not a growth phase, and it can cause serious, even permanent, damage to the body. Untreated, an eating disorder can lead to death.

The three major eating disorders are anorexia nervosa, bulimia nervosa, and binge eating disorder.

Anorexia nervosa: The main characteristics of anorexia are a persistent below-minimal weight, an intense fear of gaining weight/being fat, and having a distorted body image. In females, a fourth characteristic is amenorrhea (failure to menstruate).

Bulimia nervosa: Bulimia is characterized by repeated episodes of eating large amounts of food, followed by purging behaviors such as induced vomiting or use of laxatives. Excessive exercising to compensate for binge eating is also common.

Binge eating disorder: The primary symptom of binge eating disorder is repeated episodes of eating excessively large amounts of food, especially when not physically hungry. Unlike bulimics, binge eaters do not purge the food or try to make up for binging by exercising excessively. As a result, binge eaters are typically overweight or obese.

COMMON CHARACTERISTICS OF DIFFERENT EATING DISORDERS

	ANOREXIA	**BULIMIA**	**BINGE EATING**
Food intake	restrictive or binge/purge	binge/purge	compulsive overeating
Body weight	below minimal, emaciated	normal	usually overweight or obese
Body image	fear of being fat, distorted idea of body size	fear of being fat, distorted idea of body size	dissatisfaction with body size and/or shape
Self-esteem	low	low	low

WHO DEVELOPS EATING DISORDERS?

According to the American Academy of Pediatrics, "at least five million Americans suffer from various eating disorders: undereating, binge eating, or gorging and purging to prevent weight gain."[1] The National Eating Disorders Association estimates that between five and ten million are afflicted. What makes one person develop an eating disorder while another does not?[2]

Eating disorders occur in children, adolescents, and adults of both sexes. They occur in all social classes and races and across all economic levels. Research into exactly how many people have eating disorders and what their lifestyles are like is hampered by a key obstacle: many who suffer an eating disorder are able to hide it, not only from their doctors but from friends and family, too. These cases go unreported—and untreated. Despite this difficulty, researchers have identified certain ages and groups that seem most susceptible to eating disorders.

Most eating disorders develop in young people age twelve to eighteen, but they have been reported in younger children and in adults as old as seventy-seven. Most of these individuals are female, but 10 percent or more are males. Experts say that the number of eating disorders reported in males is growing. Some people develop an eating disorder as a teen and carry it into adulthood. Others develop an eating disorder as an adult in response to overwhelming pressures to be thin or to achieve a particular body type. Professional models, actors, dancers, and athletes are at particular risk to these pressures. Some young adults develop eating disorders as a result of the stress and pressures of college.

Eating disorders result from a combination of different factors that we can categorize as psychological, interpersonal, cultural (social), and familial (family) in nature. Of course, no one person necessarily exhibits all symptoms in a single category or in all four categories.

Psychological factors: low self-esteem, feelings of inadequacy, need for self-determination in one's life, depression, anxiety, anger, loneliness, impulsiveness.

Interpersonal factors: troubled relationships with family or friends, history of being teased or ridiculed for one's size or weight, history of physical or sexual abuse.

Cultural factors: the glorification of thinness, following the crowd, evaluating people based on appearance and not on inner qualities, skills, talents, or other strengths.

Familial factors: history of depression and/or of eating disorders, unhealthy patterns of eating, influence on personality traits.

Researchers cannot point to a particular risk factor or type of person and say with certainty that an individual is likely to develop an eating disorder. The truth is, each person's response to pressures—both external and internal—is unique. Some are able to resist or reject media messages that a rail-thin body is attractive, desirable, and healthy. Others, though, are unable to refute this message and develop a warped idea of what normal is. Not all people who develop this syndrome, however, do so in response to media messages or professional demands on body size. For some, the root of the problem is internal or familial (in the family system).

HOW IS AN EATING DISORDER TREATED?

An eating disorder is an illness that must be treated. As time passes, more and more damage is inflicted on the person's body and mental health. Every year thousands of people die due to complications from these maladies.

The good news is that eating disorders are treatable, and recovery is possible. To be effective, a treatment program must take into account the individual's state of health, both physical and psychological. The ideal source of help is an expert in treating eating disorders. For example, a psychotherapist or psychologist with special training in treating eating disorders may coordinate treatment. That doctor may link efforts with the patient's primary care physician and a nutritionist.

A treatment program addresses the symptoms of the eating disorder, the "visible" signs of illness such as emaciation or obesity. It introduces therapy to address underlying psychological, social, cultural, and/or familial issues. Such therapy helps the patient identify the internal and external factors

WHEN SOMEONE YOU KNOW HAS AN EATING DISORDER

If you think someone you know has a serious eating problem, there are a few things you can do to help. Remember, though, that it is a doctor's job to diagnose eating disorders. As a friend, your role is to show concern and to encourage your pal to talk to a qualified professional.

- Talk to your friend privately.
- Give examples of why you think your friend has an eating disorder.
- Explain why you are concerned, focusing on the person's health and relationships rather than appearance or weight.
- Listen carefully to everything your friend has to say.
- Be prepared for your companion to react with anger or denial.
- Remember that your friend's problems cannot be solved after a single conversation with you.
- Check in again after he or she has had time to think it over.
- Avoid trying to "cure" your friend by yourself.
- Offer to go with your friend to talk to a school nurse, counselor, parent, or other trusted adult.
- If your friend resists all your efforts to help, but you still suspect an eating problem, talk to a counselor, doctor, or other qualified person for guidance.

Professionals specializing in eating disorders understand the challenges their patients face.

involved in distorted body image, low self-esteem, and the impulse to restrict food or to eat compulsively.

No single "magic" course of treatment exists. For some, weekly sessions with a therapist and consultation with a medical doctor are effective. Others need treatment in a hospital, either as an outpatient or an inpatient. Such medical care is necessary, for instance, when the disorder has caused some degree of damage that calls for medical attention. Still other patients may need to live temporarily at a facility designed for the treatment of patients with similar problems.

CAN EATING DISORDERS BE PREVENTED?

The question of whether eating disorders can be prevented is tricky. Unlike the flu, these disorders don't have a vaccine—literal or figurative—that immunizes you. The strongest preventative measures are information and education.

It is important to know the factors that increase the risk of an eating disorder. These risk factors are present before visible symptoms of a disorder show up. They include a preoccupation with weight or shape, teasing from friends about one's body size or eating habits, problems at home (anything from divorce to alcoholism within the family), and dieting. Having a family member or close friend stricken with an eating disorder is another risk factor, as is having another influential figure who obsessively diets or who has an eating disorder.

Besides knowing risk factors, you should know that an eating disorder in its early stages is more easily treated than a firmly entrenched illness. For this reason, you should consider any symptoms of eating disorders as early warning bells. As listed in the chart in this chapter, some common characteristics are restricted food intake, binge eating with or without purging, and distorted body image.

Despite education and awareness of risk factors and symptoms, some influences may seem beyond our control. In spite of frequent criticism, the high-fashion and film industries continue to glorify unnatural thinness. As mistaken as it is, some coaches advise their athletes to follow unsafe diets in order to qualify for weight limits, as in wrestling, or to achieve a particular body size or weight, as in gymnastics, ballet, and ice skating. High-profile celebrities continue to use cigarettes, drugs, and fad diets to stay thin. Regarding these compelling influences, keep all things in perspective. Don't let yourself be fooled into thinking that the media reflects real life, much less healthy bodies.

Confronting an eating disorder includes working to develop a realistic perception of the body's shape and size.

Myth: *Smart people don't develop eating disorders.*
Fact: *Smart, well-educated people do develop eating disorders. An estimated 15 percent of college women meet diagnostic criteria for anorexia or bulimia.[1]*

5
EATING DISORDERS AND SELF-IMAGE

Self-image is how you regard yourself, how you assess your personal qualities, how you judge your individual worth. Your self-image includes how you perceive both your inner self—your personal thoughts and feelings—and your physical body. Of course, self-image does not develop in a vacuum. How you see yourself is influenced by culture and society and by how you think you compare with the ideals that confront you.

A healthy self-image results from a realistic perception of your inner qualities and external appearance combined with an acceptance of your uniqueness. Faced with changing cultural ideals, however, many people find it difficult to realistically evaluate who they are and what they look like. Over the past fifty to sixty years in the United States, high-fashion models and movie stars have represented ideals of body beauty. From decade to decade, though, the ideal body shape and size tend to change. Consider the measurements of the symbols of beauty over the years in the chart "The size of beauty."

How do you see yourself? To get an idea, think about the following questions.

- What kind of personality do you have?
- Do you like your personality?
- What do you think others think of your personality?
- What is your body shape and size?
- How do you think others perceive your body?
- Do you accept your body, or do you want to change it?
- What do you value about yourself (e.g., skills, talents, looks)?
- Do you think your family values your strong points? Your friends?
- Do you like who you are?
- Do you think other people tend to like you or dislike you?

The size of beauty, decade to decade

Decade	Symbol of Beauty	Bust-Waist-Hips (inches)	Height
1950s	Marilyn Monroe	37-23-36	5' 5.5"
1960s	Twiggy	32-22-32	5' 6"
1970s	Jerry Hall	36-24-36	6'
1980s	Cindy Crawford	34-24-35	5' 9.5"
1990s	Kate Moss	33-23-35	5' 8"
2000s	Heidi Klum	35-24-34	5' 9.5"

Gradually we have moved from a realistic idea of beauty, one that includes the average-sized woman, to an unrealistic idea that most women cannot attain. In the 1950s, Marilyn Monroe's height, at 5' 5.5", was near the average woman's height of 5' 4". Her body size and shape were in healthy proportion to her height. Now flash forward to the first decade of the 2000s. Fashion models are typically 5' 9" to 5' 11" in height—5 to 7 inches taller than the average woman. Despite their height, their weight is typically between 110 and 117 pounds. An average healthy teenager or adult who compares herself to fashion models will almost always find herself shorter and heavier.

BODY IMAGE

Part of your self-image is tied up in your conception of your body—your body image. What do you think of your appearance, your shape, your size, your weight? How do you think family members, friends, and strangers perceive your body? How much value do you place on their perceptions?

Most fashion models represent unrealistic ideas of the human form.

Your body image develops in response to many factors. One of these is puberty. As children enter this phase of growth, their bodies change rapidly in shape, height, and weight. Girls develop breasts and rounded hips and thighs. Boys build up more muscle and bulkier bodies. Both girls and boys grow taller and gain weight. Body fat is redistributed. If you are a girl, your chubby face may grow lean while your formerly lean hips widen and round out. These changes are normal and necessary to healthy physical development.

As if these changes weren't enough to deal with, the rate of growth varies from person to person. Some people enter puberty early and some later. When young people notice their own changes or lack of change in relation to their friends, they form opinions of their own bodies. Some individuals may feel comfortable during puberty, but most young people experience some degree of awkwardness, self-consciousness, and insecurity in relation to their bodies. This is totally normal and does not indicate a distorted body image or psychological disorder.

Another factor that influences your body image is your family's attitudes. Parents' opinions of their own bodies have a direct impact on how you see yourself. A parent who obsessively counts calories, continually tries fad diets, or bemoans every ounce of body fat sends a message that thinness is success/good and fatness is failure/bad. Family nicknames and teasing play important roles, too. A child who grows up being called chubby may have difficulty thinking of himself any other way, even if he achieves a healthy weight. A child who is affectionately called string bean may take pleasure in the nickname and feel her body is betraying her when it matures into a rounded adult shape. Siblings, too, influence one another's body image and can carelessly use barbed teasing or cutting insults that cause lasting pain and self-doubt.

What is more, young people of your own age are an important and influential part of your life, helping you on the road to independence, giving you a sense of belonging, and sometimes understanding you better than your family. For these reasons, your peers—both friends and enemies—have a massive influence on your self-image. Some peers may accept you just as you are. Their attitudes help strengthen or build up your satisfaction with your body. On the other hand, some teens may tease you, imply that you should lose weight, or joke about your lack of muscles. These kinds of opinions and comments can be painful and difficult to ignore or reject and can increase your dissatisfaction with your body.

As discussed earlier, the media influences people's body images. Consider the findings of researchers Jane D. Brown and Elizabeth M. Witherspoon, published in their article "The Mass Media and American Adolescents' Health."[2]

• "Food, typically sweet snacks, are consumed or referred to three to five times per half hour on prime-time programming."

• "More than two thirds of women characters on television but only 18% of the men are thin."

• "The very act of attending to the media, because it requires no physical effort, contributes to weight gain."

• "Models used to weigh about 8% less than the 'average' woman; now they weigh about 23% less."

• "Analyses of body measurements from 500 models listed on modeling agency Web sites and from Playboy centerfolds from 1985 to 1997 showed that nearly all the centerfolds and three fourths of the models had body mass indexes (BMI) of 17.5 or below—the American Psychological Association's criterion for anorexia nervosa."

All of these factors—puberty, family, peers, and mass media—contribute to how you see your body. The most significant factor, though, in the development of your body image is you. A healthy body image is achievable.

A HEALTHY BODY IMAGE

Your body image does not spring forth overnight. Rather, it develops slowly over time and in response to many influences, such as those discussed here. In the same way, building your satisfaction with your body takes time. To develop a healthier body image, start with where you are and work from there. Here are some suggestions.

Suggestions for Improving Your Body Image

- Think about the factors that have helped define your body image, from childhood through the present.
- Give your body the nutrition, exercise, and rest it needs to be healthy.
- Take a break from television, films, and magazines. Spend more time with real people.
- Choose friends who accept you as you are.
- Pick a type of physical activity and do it—just for fun!
- Get rid of the bathroom scales. Evaluate your body based on how you are taking care of yourself with nutrition and physical activity, not by how much you weigh.
- Join efforts with family and peers to learn more about what is healthy and what is destructive to body image.
- Spend time getting to know your inner self—what your strengths are, what you like and dislike, who you are becoming as a person.
- Remember that fabulous people come in all shapes and sizes. You don't have to look like "everyone else" to be acceptable, lovable, attractive, or productive.

A key difference between a healthy and an unhealthy body image is being realistic about how you see yourself. Judging yourself by unreasonable standards can lead to unhealthy patterns of eating, depression, low self-esteem, and other problems. In more extreme cases, a poor or distorted body image can lead to harmful weight-control behaviors and eating disorders.

In order to see your body realistically, you need factual

information, not fake messages and images that manipulate your emotions and distort your perceptions. In one study, university researchers found that over 33 percent of female students and 25 percent of male students considered themselves to be overweight.[3] However, it is estimated that only 10—15 percent of children and adolescents are overweight.[4] Knowing what a healthy body weight is for you is one way to turn your focus to health, nutrition, and fitness and away from a fun-house distorted body image. Healthy body weight is the subject of the next chapter.

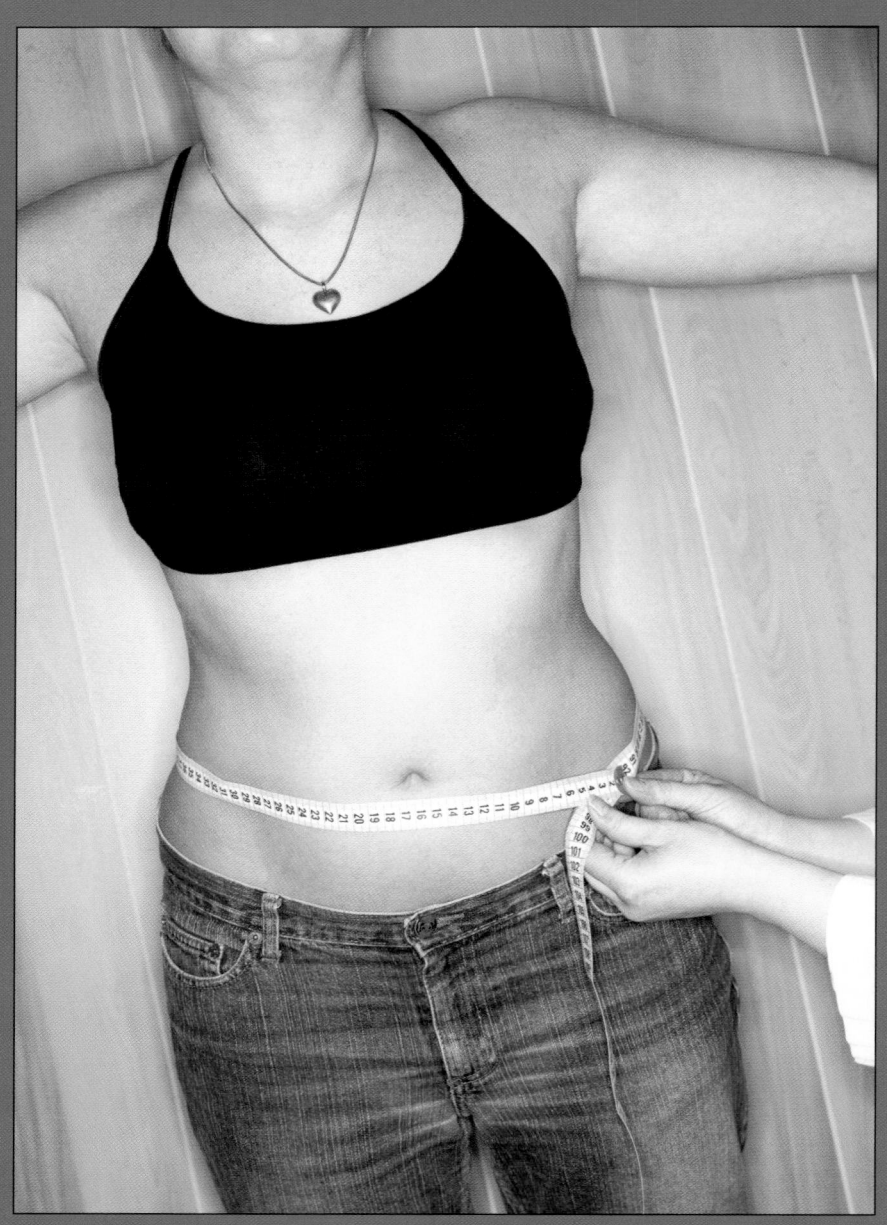

Healthy bodies come in an endless array of shapes, sizes, and weights.

6
BODY WEIGHT

Studies reveal that approximately 40 percent or more of all adolescents are trying to lose weight.[1] Are all of these young people overweight? Not at all. In fact, only about 10 to 15 percent of children and adolescents are overweight.[2]

When it comes to assessing your own weight, how do you know whether you are at a healthy weight? It helps to consult body mass index (BMI) charts or height/weight charts. These tables use standards established by doctors and other professionals to provide guidelines to the general population. Bear in mind, though, that no two bodies are alike in their distribution of bone, muscle, and fat. Lifestyle and genetics also have a hand in what you weigh. Learning about all these factors will help you determine a healthy body weight for yourself.

BODY FAT

Everybody, male or female, needs fat stores to remain healthy and to function efficiently. Fat supplies energy and is necessary for cell membrane structure, blood-clotting processes, and the transportation of fat-soluble vitamins. Individuals who try to rid their bodies of all fat can harm or permanently damage their bodies. For instance, when a female who has gone through puberty falls below about

22 percent body fat, her body may stop menstruating (getting a period every month). If she begins eating healthfully and regains the necessary body fat, her period will usually resume.

So how much body fat do you have right now? How much do you need, and how much is too much?

To determine precisely how much fat your body is storing right now, you could get a professional body fat analysis. This type of test requires special equipment to weigh a person underwater. Another kind of professional test uses a method called X-ray absorptiometry to measure body fat. These tests are the most accurate, but they are expensive and can be inconvenient for the average person.

Another way to measure body fat is to use a method recommended by the National Institutes of Health. This can be done on your own, without special equipment. The method takes into account your body mass index, your waist measurement in inches, and your individual medical history.

BODY MASS INDEX

Your body mass index (BMI) is calculated using only your weight and your height. This index number estimates what your body fat is in relation to your height. To determine your BMI, take your weight in pounds and divide that number by your height in inches squared. Multiply that number by 703. The mathematical formula looks like this:

$$\text{BMI} = \left(\frac{\text{weight in pounds}}{(\text{height in inches}) \times (\text{height in inches})} \right) \times 703$$

For example, suppose a high school girl weighs 140 pounds and is 5' 4" tall. Her BMI would be 24. A boy who weighs 155 pounds and stands 5' 10" tall has a BMI of 22.2.

A healthy BMI falls in the range of 18.5–24.9. A BMI of less than 18.5 is considered underweight; a BMI between 25 and 29.9 is considered overweight; a BMI of 30 or greater is considered obese.

BMI	Healthy			Overweight			Obese			
	19	22	24	25	27	29	30	33	36	39
Height	Body Weight (pounds)									
4'10"	91	105	115	119	129	138	143	158	172	186
4'11"	94	109	119	124	133	143	148	163	178	193
5'0"	97	112	123	128	138	148	153	168	184	199
5'1"	100	116	127	132	143	153	158	174	190	206
5'2"	104	120	131	136	147	158	164	180	196	213
5'3"	107	124	135	141	152	163	169	186	203	220
5'4"	110	128	140	145	157	169	174	192	209	227
5'5'	114	132	144	150	162	174	180	198	216	234
5'6"	118	136	148	155	167	179	186	204	223	241
5'7"	121	140	153	159	172	185	191	211	230	249
5'8"	125	144	158	164	177	190	197	216	236	256
5'9"	128	149	162	169	182	196	203	223	243	263
5'10"	132	153	167	174	188	202	209	229	250	271
5'11"	136	157	172	179	193	208	215	236	257	279
6'0"	140	162	177	184	199	213	221	242	265	287
6'1"	144	166	182	189	204	219	227	250	272	295
6'2"	148	171	186	194	210	225	233	256	280	303

Source: Adapted from National Heart, Lung, and Blood Institute, "Body Mass Index Table."

A METRIC CALCULATION OF THE BMI FORMULA IS FOUND ON PAGE 106.

Using your figures, find your BMI in the BMI reference chart to see if your BMI falls within a healthy range for your height and weight.

If you are age twenty or younger, you can turn to Appendix A or B in this book and use your BMI and age to determine your BMI-for-age percentile.

The BMI number gives a good indication of a person's

amount of stored body fat. The BMI formula does not distinguish, however, between body weight measured from muscle and body weight from fat. Some heavily muscled athletes may have a BMI in the unhealthy range when in fact they are not overweight. You should also take into account your waist measurement and your personal medical history when evaluating your body weight.

WAIST MEASUREMENT

Some of the health problems associated with being overweight or obese are high blood pressure, diabetes, abnormal levels of blood fats, and coronary artery disease. Measuring the circumference of your waist can help you evaluate your health. Determine whether your body tends to store excess fat around your waist and upper body or around your thighs and lower body. Excess fat in the waist/abdominal area carries a greater risk of health problems than fat stored lower in the body.

The most useful waist measurement is to measure your abdomen just above the hip bones. A measurement greater than 40 inches for men or 35 inches for women indicates excess fat stored in the abdominal area. Because this body type is round in the middle, it is often referred to as "apple shaped." Apple-shaped bodies have a higher risk of fat-related health problems than "pear-shaped" bodies, the ones that store fat lower down.

MEDICAL HISTORY

A third approach to evaluating health in relation to body weight is to consider personal medical history. A family history of obesity, cardiovascular disease, diabetes, or high blood pressure indicates that you are at higher risk for developing such a health problem. Being overweight increases this risk.

There are medical causes of being overweight, though they do not occur frequently. One cause is low thyroid function. The thyroid gland regulates the speed or energy at which cells in the body work. If thyroid levels decrease, activity in the body slows down, causing excess energy to be stored as fat even though the person may be eating a healthful diet. Another medical cause of weight gain is Cushing's syndrome, a hormonal disorder caused by prolonged exposure to high levels of the hormone cortisol. It is most common in adults aged twenty to fifty and occurs in only about ten or fifteen of every million people. A medical doctor is needed to diagnose these disorders.

Many young people wonder if they are destined to follow a family history of overweight or obesity. The answer to this question is not simple. Researchers report a tendency for obesity to run in families, but they caution that the connection between genetics and obesity is inconclusive. A person may become overweight or obese because of family eating and lifestyle habits, not because of genetics.

A family that routinely eats large portions of fatty foods, for example, especially fast foods and junk foods, is more likely to be overweight than a family that eats reasonable portions of grains, lean meats, vegetables, and fruits. To an outside observer it may look as if one family is genetically programmed to be fat and the other is not, but a realistic look at their patterns of eating suggests otherwise.

In addition to genetic factors, your personal medical history includes your lifestyle factors. If you are routinely active physically, you will use more energy from the food you eat. As a result, your body will store less energy as fat. In contrast, sitting at a desk in school or an office is being sedentary, basically inactive. Sedentary persons are more likely to have excess body fat.

Each year in the United States, state health departments collect data about obesity among its residents. The Centers for Disease Control and Prevention compiles all the data to determine the prevalence of obesity in the country. In 2004 seven states reported that 15–19 percent of their residents were obese. In thirty-three states, 20–24 percent of residents were obese. Nine states reported that 25 percent or more of their residents were obese—that's at least one in four people! (No data was collected for Hawaii.)[3]

As the nationwide trend toward obesity grows, researchers put increasing effort into identifying lifestyle factors that support high body weights. Some studies have probed television watching. In "Children's Television and Nutrition: Friends or Foes?" Gina Pazzaglia Sylvester and her colleagues suggest that TV-related factors influencing viewers' eating habits include the following:

• The foods most advertised on TV are sweets, snacks, sweetened breakfast cereals, and beverages (such as soda).
• Prime-time programs include more representations of food than commercials do.
• The number of overweight/obese characters depicted in children's and adult programs is much lower than the number of actually overweight/obese people in real life.[4]

One of researchers' greatest concerns is that watching television is a sedentary activity (not to mention the habitual snacking while watching). On average, children and adolescents spend three hours a day watching TV.[5] One study, however, found that young people who watched four or more hours per day of TV had the highest body mass indexes (BMIs). In contrast, those who watched less than one hour of TV per day had the lowest BMIs.[6]

Does watching television make you fat? Researchers would say that being sedentary leads to weight problems. Watching television is one way of being sedentary.

WHEN BODY WEIGHT BECOMES A PROBLEM

Using the information and tools in this chapter, you can assess your BMI, waist measurement, and medical history. These three resources together help determine whether your body is at a healthy weight. If your BMI is between 18.5 and 24.9, and your waist measurement is less than 40 inches (for men) or 35 inches (for women), and your medical history raises no red flags, then you are likely at a healthy body weight.

If your BMI is 18.5 or lower, you are probably underweight. A low BMI of this sort is often an indication of an eating disorder and should not be dismissed. Evaluation by a medical doctor is essential. The next chapter in this book, Anorexia Nervosa, gives more information about that eating disorder, which is associated with a low BMI.

Similarly, if your BMI is 25 or greater and your waist measurement is over 40 inches (for men) or 35 inches (for women), you are likely to be overweight. If your BMI is 30 or greater, you are likely obese. You may or may not have a family history of weight problems. In either case, your weight places you at risk for many health problems, and a consultation with your doctor is in order. For more information about an eating disorder associated with overweight and obesity, consult chapter nine, Binge Eating Disorder.

Even if your BMI and waist measurements fall within healthy ranges, it is essential to evaluate your medical history carefully, especially if you feel dissatisfied with your weight. Not all eating disorders result in a low or a high BMI or produce risky waist measurements. Someone suffering from bulimia, for example, may have a body of apparently healthy weight and size yet practice disordered patterns of eating that cause health risks. Chapter eight tells more about bulimia nervosa. As with other points of concern regarding weight, it is wise to consult a doctor if you want help assessing or accepting your weight.

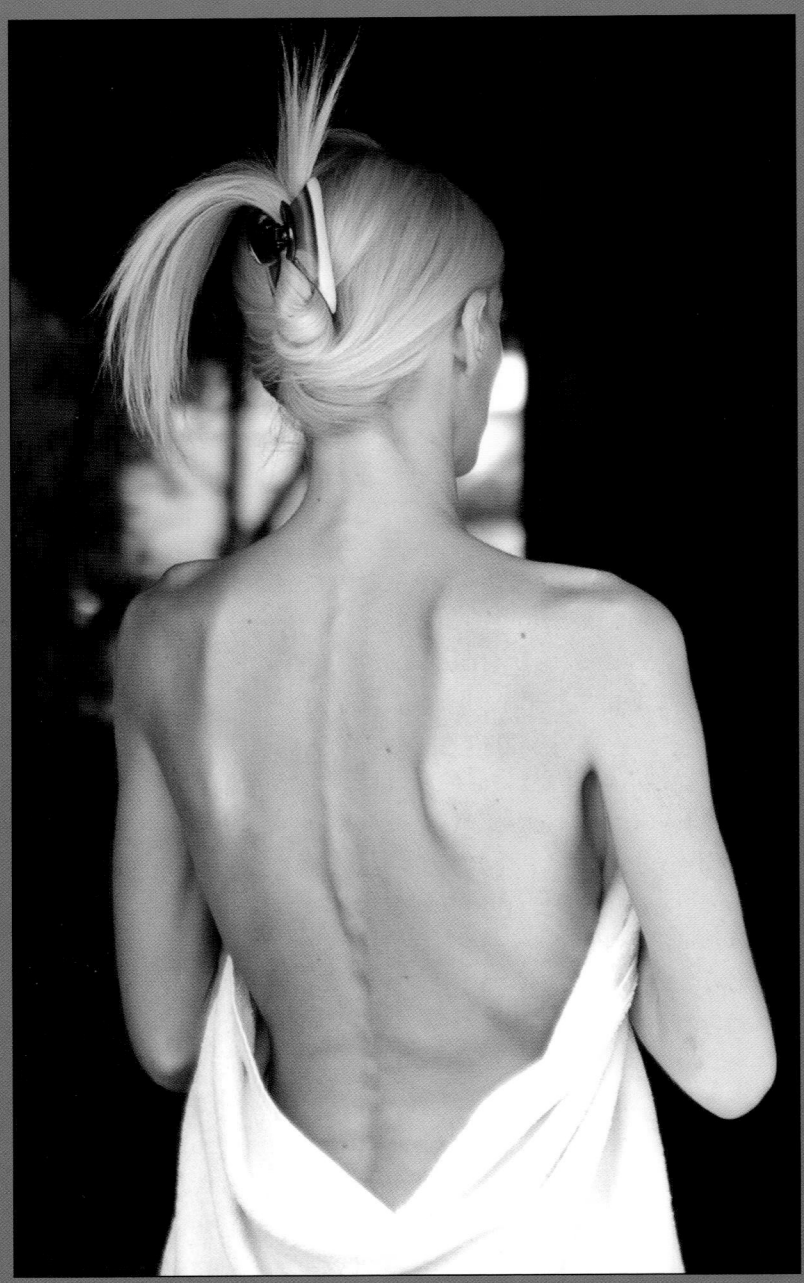

Despite mounting pressure to represent realistic body sizes in the media, a visibly fat-free body persists as a standard of beauty for countless people worldwide.

Myth: *Anorexia is a girl's problem.*
Fact: *Most anorexics are female, but about 10 percent or more are male.*[1]

7
ANOREXIA NERVOSA

Anorexia nervosa, usually just called anorexia, is a medical condition in which the most evident symptom is extremely low body weight. Individuals with anorexia are obsessed with being thin. They see themselves as fat when, in fact, they are extremely skinny or emaciated. Anorexic people spend a great deal of effort avoiding food and situations in which they are expected to eat. During family mealtimes, school lunch periods, or parties with food, they find ways to avoid eating, to hide the food they supposedly ate, or to make excuses for why they are not eating. When they do eat, however tiny the amount is, they choose extremely low-calorie foods, such as celery, and diet soda drinks. To these people, eating in itself can feel disgusting or frightening. Some anorexic victims force themselves to throw up the food they ate. Others may exercise for long periods of time to burn off all or more than the calories they consumed.

These patterns of behaviors cause the person's body weight and body mass index (BMI) to fall dangerously low. Even though he or she appears gaunt or sick, the person feels a powerful aversion to eating or gaining weight and persists in dangerous behavior.

Given this preoccupation with food and weight, it is easy to assume that anorexia is all about looks—looking as thin as a fashion model or being the thinnest person in the classroom. Anorexia is a medical illness, however, not vanity. Typically, the disease results from the afflicted person's attempt to use food and body weight to control problems in his or her life. Anorexia involves both the physical and the mental health of those who suffer from it. Additionally, the sufferer may be unaware of which life problems are fueling the anorexia. Many anorexics feel powerless against the illness that afflicts them.

The symptoms of anorexia include more than just extreme weight loss. In a child who is still growing, anorexia can show up as a failure to gain the needed weight to develop normally, as opposed to losing weight. In effect, the child's body freezes in childhood rather than maturing naturally into adolescence. A girl in this situation is unlikely to begin menstruating. The following lists these and other symptoms of anorexia.

SOME PHYSICAL SYMPTOMS OF ANOREXIA NERVOSA

- Body weight that is about 20 percent below normal.
- Downy (soft and fluffy) hair on the face and arms.
- Dry, scaly skin.
- Fainting.
- Frequent scratches or cuts on knuckles (from forced vomiting).
- In females, irregular periods or no periods (amenorrhea).

Anorexia most often occurs in teenage girls, but boys, too, may develop anorexia. While female sufferers tend to focus on reducing their body size as much as possible, males often combine starvation practices with attempts to build muscle or achieve an athletic appearance. Some young people take their anorexia with them into college and into their twenties. At any age, anorexia is destructive to the person's health and should be regarded as a medical priority.

MEDICAL CONSEQUENCES

Death is the most extreme consequence of anorexia. Anywhere from five to nineteen of every one hundred anorexics die due to health problems that arise from starving themselves.[2] Among anorexics whose disease has gone untreated, the death rate is closer to 25 percent. It is important to note that clinical anorexia nervosa is a rare disorder. It is estimated that the disease afflicts only about 0.5 to 3 percent of the general population—that is, three or fewer people per one hundred.[3]

However, not all people who practice the behaviors of anorexia have clinical cases of the disorder. Some of these sufferers get professional help and regain healthy patterns of eating and thinking. Others in this borderline category are unable to cope and eventually become clinically (officially) diagnosed with anorexia. One study suggests that up to 22 percent of college-age women practice some form of anorexic behavior.[4] All of these individuals—both diagnosed and undiagnosed—face serious medical consequences from their starvation behaviors.

What are these medical consequences? The most obvious is malnutrition. Someone who severely restricts his or her food intake is unable to get the necessary nutrients to keep the body in healthy working order. For example, people weighing 15 percent less than the normal weight for their height are unlikely to have enough body fat for necessary body processes.[5] At 20 percent below a healthy weight for their height, many anorexic individuals weigh even less than that.

When the body does not receive enough nutrition, it begins shutting down. Essential bodily processes become sluggish. Blood pressure drops, the pulse slows, and breathing gets slower. As a result, sufferers may feel lightheaded or may faint. They may find it difficult to concentrate in school or to focus their attention on a conversation. Not eating enough can damage the heart, the liver, and the kidneys.

Other problems include swollen joints and brittle bones. The person's scalp hair may begin to thin or fall out, while a downy hair grows on the face and arms. Anorexia can include anemia—a reduced level of red blood cells, which are essential for carrying oxygen throughout the body. A girl whose period stops (or never begins in the first place) due to anorexia can face long-term problems such as osteoporosis.

PSYCHOLOGICAL PATTERNS OF ANOREXICS

Besides physical problems, anorexia involves painful and confusing psychological problems. One of the most common is misperception about the body. Sufferers see themselves as fat, pudgy, or heavy when an objective observer sees clearly that they are not. Despite reassurances of their slimness or the data on a BMI or height/weight chart, they still feel fat. Alternatively, they may concede that certain body parts are okay, such as thin cheeks, but other body parts are still fat— the abdomen or thighs, for example.

These misperceptions about body size, weight, and shape can result in deep embarrassment or shame regarding the body. The sufferer may habitually wear baggy clothes to hide the body. They may avoid playing sports at school that require revealing clothing such as swimming suits or shorts.

Despite their reluctance to actually eat, anorexic individuals often develop elaborate rituals associated with food. They may spend hours in the kitchen each week, cooking and baking for the family. At mealtime they say they ate while cooking or got full by snacking on ingredients. They may spend time exchanging recipes with others and trying out new recipes but always give away everything they make. Some people may hoard food and yet refuse to eat it, even in response to painful feelings of starvation.

In some cases the severe restriction of food intake becomes too hard to keep up. Sufferers may consume large amounts of food in one sitting and then, overcome by guilt, shame, disgust, or stomach pain, force themselves to throw up. This binge-purge behavior is true of people with bulimia, too. The difference is that people with anorexia are far below a healthy body weight, while those with bulimia may appear at or above a healthy body weight.

People with anorexia may feel compelled to burn off calories from the food they have eaten. They may walk, jog, or run for long periods of time and become upset if they are kept from their routine. Just as some people develop food rituals, some others develop exercise rituals: jogging a certain number of miles, climbing a certain number of steps, or burning off a certain number of calories per day. They refuse to take a day off for bad weather, holidays, illness, or even injury. If someone attempts to persuade them to take a break, or circumstances force them to disrupt their ritual, they become angry.

This obsession with exercise is sometimes used to deny the presence of the eating disorder. How could I have an eating disorder and still have the energy to work out the way I do? To complicate matters, our society is programmed to admire and reward people who achieve extreme levels of fitness. Compulsive exercising is easily accepted as an admirable act of self-discipline and health.

Routine social situations can pose problems for those with anorexia. Trips with friends to the mall food court or a coffee shop can cause anxiety. A simple birthday party where everyone is served cake can bring about frustration or panic. The person feels unable to eat with the others but is unwilling to attract attention by refusing food. The victim may hide the food in a napkin and throw it into the garbage or flush it down the toilet. He or she may take bites of food but then spit them out into a cup (while pretending to drink) or into a napkin. An event that was supposed to be fun becomes an exercise in food rejection. To avoid facing such difficulties and to prevent friends' noticing their refusal to eat, anorexics may cut down on or eliminate social activities altogether. This restriction increases loneliness, self-doubt, anxiety, and depression, all unhappy consequences.

TREATMENT OF ANOREXIA NERVOSA

Anorexia can be treated. The first priority of treatment is to help the person begin eating nutritiously and gaining necessary weight. Closely tied to this priority is helping the patient confront and deal with the psychological conflicts that contribute to the anorexic behaviors. Third, the person's disordered behaviors must be replaced with nondestructive ones.

Health-care professionals who treat people with anorexia include psychiatrists (they are medical doctors), psychologists, nutritionists, social workers, occupational therapists (they specialize in psychosocial therapy), and nurses. These people may have completed special training in the assessment and treatment of anorexia. They each bring specific skills to the treatment process and may work as a team treating the same patient.

One of the first issues to deal with when a person begins treatment is whether he or she needs to be hospitalized. Hospitalization is necessary when the patient's symptoms are life threatening or when a psychological evaluation determines that the patient needs hospitalization to begin recovery. It is important to recognize that seeking treatment for anorexia is by far not an easy thing for people to do. They may feel ambivalent about getting better. They realize they need outside help, but gaining weight to get better seems like an impossible task. Some patients need a hospital setting to get started on recovery.

Other patients are able to begin treatment as an outpatient, meaning they do not check into a hospital. Instead, they have regular appointments with the professionals who are providing treatment. If an outpatient is not able to begin eating better and gaining weight, he or she may need hospitalization.

For inpatient or outpatient treatment alike, one of the patient's first goals is gaining weight. Females need to gain enough weight to resume their regular monthly periods. All patients need to put on enough weight to allow their bodies to grow, develop, and function normally.

For hospitalized patients, a target weight gain may be two to three pounds per week. "Force feeding," such as intravenous or tube feeding, is ordinarily used only when the patient's life is in danger. For outpatients, the target is typically half a pound to a pound a week. As patients gain weight, they are monitored for possible complications. They also receive education about how to choose foods, form a healthy diet plan, and incorporate reasonable physical activity. They may be advised to keep a journal to record food intake and related behaviors such as forced vomiting or laxative use. All this is part of learning healthy patterns of eating.

For people with anorexia, putting on weight takes willingness and cooperation on their part. To help patients change old, harmful ideas about weight and body size, therapy is crucial. Therapists help patients understand why they need treatment, including weight gain, and help patients learn to change their behaviors, including taking part in social situations that have been challenging in the past. In conjunction with all this, psychological therapy helps patients identify and deal with problems that contribute to their anorexia.

In some cases family members need to receive therapy, too, especially younger teens in the family. The disorder may have developed in response to a patient's relationship with a parent, aunt, grandparent, or other relative. Family members, however well-intentioned, may in fact be supporting the disorder with attitudes, words, or actions. Another reason for family therapy is to provide help and information to family members themselves. They may feel shame, guilt, anger, confusion, or any number of emotions related to the patient's anorexia. Family therapists help the family as a whole so that everyone can change and heal.

Medication may be—but is not always—incorporated into the treatment program, usually after the patient has gained weight. To treat depression, anxiety, or obsessive-compulsive behaviors, antidepressants or tranquilizers may be prescribed. Medication is often prescribed together with other modes of treatment, including the medical, behavioral, and psychological therapies discussed above.

Treatment takes time and patience, and relapses are common. The American Academy of Pediatrics estimates that about a third of patients with anorexia "have long-term problems coping with food and accepting a normal weight."[6] The starvation practices of the disorder may have damaged the patient's body in ways that have lifelong effects. Experts estimate that 5 percent to 19 percent or more of patients with anorexia die sooner than they would have without the disease, usually as a result of heart attack or suicide.[7] Specialists emphasize that the sooner a person gets treatment for the disorder, the better his or her chances of recovery and survival are.

EATING DISORDERS AND THE INTERNET

If you type "eating disorder" into an Internet search engine, you will get a staggering array of links to pages of data, FAQs, research findings, online counseling, advertisements for treatment providers or facilities, discussion boards, chat rooms, and more.

Some of these sites are reliable, accurate, and trustworthy; others are not. A few unfortunate sites, called proanorexia Web sites, actually promote anorexia, offering tips and encouragement for maintaining the disorder. Despite proanorexia sites' efforts to wrap anorexia in pretty packaging, remember that anorexia is not a party game, a secret club, or a fun thing to try out. It is a serious disorder that can—and does—kill you.

How can you tell whether a Web site is trustworthy and accurate? Check to see who or what organization created the site. Sites created by government health services (look for URLs ending in ".gov") and by recognized eating disorder organizations are usually reliable. Other reliable sites are maintained by college or university health services departments (look for ".edu" at the end of the URL). Sites that are written by a single person not affiliated with an accredited professional organization are less reliable. Although there are exceptions, one-creator sites are more likely to include one-sided opinions, misinformation, inaccurate data/information, and out-of-date material.

Names of some trustworthy Web sites and eating disorder organizations are included in the back of this book.

While most people suffering from bulimia appear to be of normal size and weight, they experience intense internal conflict over body image.

> **Myth:** *Bulimia is not that bad—after all, you probably won't die from it.*
>
> **Fact:** *Although fewer than 1 percent of bulimics die from the disorder,[1] it results in damage to the teeth, esophagus, stomach, lungs, heart, and kidneys. Bulimic women may have problems becoming pregnant or carrying a baby to term.*

8
BULIMIA NERVOSA

Bulimia nervosa, or bulimia, is an eating disorder characterized by cycles of binging and purging. The person eats large amounts of food in one sitting, to the point of causing stomach discomfort, and then uses some technique to force the food out of the body. Self-induced vomiting and the use of laxatives or diuretics are typical choices. Like people with anorexia, people with bulimia fixate on food, body size, and body weight. Their self-worth and body image are tied to how thin they see themselves. Unlike people with anorexia, however, those with bulimia tend to maintain a body weight that is close to normal for their height. Their body size may appear a little thin, a little plump, or completely average.

Not all people with bulimia engage in purging behaviors. Bulimics fall into two groups: those who binge and then use some method to purge the food (about 80 percent of bulimics), and those who binge but do not purge (about 20 percent). Sufferers in either group may use fasting and excessive exercising to compensate for their binging.

Bulimia occurs mainly in females, though some males manifest the disorder, too. This disorder typically develops in girls during their late teens or early twenties. Some people in their early teens, however, suffer from bulimia as well. Since most people with bulimia hide their binge/purge behaviors, it is difficult to determine how many people are actually affected. It is estimated that between 1.1 to 4.2 percent of teenagers and adults have bulimia.[2]

THE BINGE/PURGE CYCLE

Although not all people with bulimia use purging, the dominant characteristic of the disorder is the binge/purge cycle. People with bulimia experience an overwhelming urge to devour large quantities of food, often those that seem forbidden or unhealthy. They may consume a quart of ice cream, a pizza with lots of toppings, a bag of cookies, a quart of soda, a chocolate cake, and a bag of potato chips all in one sitting. Foods may be chosen because they are easy to gulp down and easy to throw up. The binging takes place within a limited period of time, such as two hours, in which the bulimic may consume 3,000 calories or more. In contrast, a healthy teenager typically consumes about 2,000 to 3,000 calories in an entire day.

This compulsion to gorge is not necessarily in response to hunger. Rather, it is driven by feelings of anxiety, tension, powerlessness, or other emotions. Someone in the grasp of a clinical case of bulimia binges at least twice a week for three months or more. On average, a bulimic binges at least once a day and often more.

When the urge to gorge fades away, strong feelings of guilt, shame, depression, sadness, or frustration set in. The person's stomach may be stretched out from the large quantities of food it contains, and the stomach may ache.

These painful emotional and physical responses provoke an overwhelming urge to get rid of the food that was eaten—and the powerful feelings of disgust. Forced vomiting is a common purging technique. The person sticks fingers down the throat to force vomiting, doing this until feeling cleansed of the food. Because of an obsession with calories and weight, the patient may feel a sense of relief that the calories are gone from the body and that the food will not add any weight. Most likely he or she gathers the food packages and wrappers and disposes of them secretly or away from home.

Some people with bulimia use laxatives or diuretics, perhaps in combination with self-induced vomiting. Laxatives force the body to speed up the process of expelling solid waste through the bowels. Similarly, diuretics induce the body to expel liquids as urine. Since laxatives and diuretics cause a drop in weight, people often feel relief that the episode of binging had no lasting results. However, the "weight loss" is mainly a loss of water, not a loss of body fat. Laxatives do not prevent the body from absorbing calories from the food and drinks. Also, the body naturally regains its stores of liquid. In the meantime, however, the body can become dehydrated.

People with bulimia may use other methods to compensate for episodes of binging. Some develop a strict exercise ritual such as biking a predetermined number of miles, climbing a certain number of flights of stairs, or jogging a specific number of miles for each episode of binging. They may keep careful charts of calories consumed and calories burned off in exercise. They may weigh themselves before and after a workout session, hoping that any weight gained from gorging will have been burned off. Some turn to drugs such as cocaine or amphetamines. Others force themselves to endure long periods of starvation to compensate for binging. Excessive exercise and starvation often backfire, causing hunger pangs that lead to another episode of binging.

The following list shows some of the physical symptoms of bulimia.

- Frequent scratches or cuts on knuckles (from forced vomiting).
- Erosion of the enamel on teeth (from stomach acid).
- Swollen glands in the neck and face.
- Stomach pain.
- Sore throats.
- Chronic heartburn.

MEDICAL CONSEQUENCES

Even though people with bulimia may have a normal body weight and body mass index, their bodies are not necessarily healthy. Binge/purge behaviors cause serious and sometimes irreversible damage. Possible medical consequences include damage to the teeth, esophagus, stomach, lungs, heart, and kidneys. Complications from such medical problems can result in death.

Vomiting causes bile and acid from the stomach to come up into the mouth. In effect, the teeth get an acid bath. Over time, acids erode the teeth's enamel and dentin, leading to serious dental problems. Frequent vomiting can also injure or rupture the esophagus. This vital tube is meant to carry food from the mouth down to the stomach. When vomiting forces bile and acids up into this tube, these stomach acids, which normally break down and digest food, irritate and burn the mucous membrane that lines the esophagus. One result is chronic heartburn (also called acid reflux). Another possible result is esophagitis, an inflammation of the esophagus. The inflammation may narrow the esophagus, making swallowing or vomiting food more difficult. The esophagus can become scarred or torn. A bleeding or ruptured esophagus is life threatening, and immediate medical attention is necessary.

The stomach itself can be harmed by binging and

vomiting. Frequent vomiting can inflame the lining of the stomach, a condition called gastritis. If the person does not vomit, the stomach is left with larger quantities of food than it is designed to process effectively at one time. Though rare, a "stuffed" stomach of this sort can rupture and cause death from peritonitis, an inflammation of the membrane lining the abdominal cavity.

Another result of frequent vomiting is the aspiration (inhaling) of food particles, gastric acid, and bacteria from the stomach into the lungs. Pneumonia can result.

Fasting, frequent vomiting, or overuse of laxatives causes the body to lose necessary fluids and electrolytes. Electrolytes are ions such as sodium, potassium, and chloride that help cells regulate the flow of water molecules across cell membranes. An imbalance in electrolytes can lead to disturbances in heart rhythm, kidney stones, and kidney failure.

Bulimia is not just a physical disorder. The person's mental health, too, is at issue.

PSYCHOLOGICAL PATTERNS OF BULIMICS

People with bulimia find it difficult to regard their bodies realistically. Their self-esteem is tied to a distorted perception of their body size and weight. A young woman whose body is at a healthy weight may see herself as fat. In fact, one of the driving motivations for binge/purge behaviors is a morbid dread of getting fat combined with an urge to gorge. People suffering with bulimia may fear that once they begin eating, they will be unable to stop. Food, therefore, frequently takes center stage in their thoughts and actions. They spend a great deal of time thinking about food, shopping for food, preparing meals, and analyzing the results of eating on their bodies. They feel simultaneously driven to eat and guilty because of eating.

Like people with anorexia, they may stay away from social

situations that include food, such as family parties or trips to a food court with friends. Some avoid eating in front of others entirely, going all day without food. At night, to make up for the starvation, they stuff themselves in private. Some bulimics are always on a weight-loss diet, a cheerless pattern broken only by periodic episodes of binging.

Bulimia indicates deeper problems than a simple desire to be thin. Many people would like to be thin, and this desire is not a disorder. Most people are able to manage their wish for thinness without developing an eating disorder and are able to separate the problems in their lives from their physical appearance. In contrast, bulimics tend to see their appearance as the cause of their problems. By blaming their problems on their body weight or size, they escape dealing with them. Instead, they fixate on food and seek relief from conflicts through bulimic patterns of behavior.

Although people with bulimia share similar symptoms, they are not alike in every way. There is no single personality type that is typical of this disorder. One person with bulimia may be outgoing, goal-oriented, and successful in school. Another may be shy, disorganized, and unsuccessful in school. Bulimia can develop in people who have low self-esteem, but it can also develop in people who have grand ideas of their own importance. Some bulimics may seek out a great deal of attention socially, while others try to hide. While not true of all with the disorder, bulimics who engage in purging behaviors tend also to exhibit other destructive behaviors, such as alcohol abuse, more than bulimics who do not purge.

TREATMENT OF BULIMIA NERVOSA

Like other eating disorders, bulimia is treatable. The chief priority is to help sufferers recognize and separate body image distortions from other conflicts in their lives. They must learn not to blame their appearance for their problems.

Instead, they must address each set of challenges—body-image problems and life problems—on its own merits. To this end, psychological and nutritional therapy have proven to be more successful in the treatment of bulimia than support groups, such as Overeaters Anonymous, alone.

A psychiatrist or psychologist trained in treating people with eating disorders can provide counseling and therapy. To plan the treatment, the therapist evaluates the patient's cognitive development. Cognition involves aspects of perception, reasoning, and judgment. During this evaluation and other psychological assessments, the patient's misperceptions, illogical reasoning, and distorted judgments become evident. The therapist is able to use these revelations as starting points for treatment.

Since a young person's family strongly influences his or her self-image and body image, treatment may include family therapy. Even young adults who have left home may still take new cues from parents or siblings in forming perceptions of

Family therapy treats the familial system, not the patient in isolation.

their bodies or in handling conflicts. In some cases the patient's bulimia nervosa may be rooted in conflicts within the family. Similarly, a married patient may, along with his or her spouse, take part in marriage therapy.

Equally important for the recovering bulimic is learning to eat when hungry and to stop when satiated, instead of eating in response to emotions. Psychological issues relating to the urge to binge are treated. Patients receive guidance in recognizing and eliminating destructive behaviors such as induced vomiting and misuse of laxatives. To replace outworn, harmful habits, patients begin to discover healthy behaviors. They learn how to solve problems and to cope with challenging situations without turning to food.

A nutritional counselor may work with the therapist to address nutritional needs and to teach healthy patterns of eating. Such a specialist helps the patient develop realistic meal and snack plans that fit within normal daily routines at home, school, and work. The patient may use a food journal to record meals, snacks, and exercise, as well as times when the urge to binge on food feels overwhelming. One goal in this part of treatment may be to include former "binge foods" in the diet, but in healthy portions and at planned meal or snack times.

In most cases people with bulimia are able to begin treatment without hospitalization. Patients who do not make progress as an outpatient, however, may require hospitalization to start getting better. Some bulimics need hospitalization due to severe psychological problems, such as suicidal tendencies or medical complications from binging, purging, or starvation practices.

Occasionally a patient's doctor may prescribe medications to help with recovery. Antidepressant medications may be used to treat symptoms of depression, anxiety, or impulse disorders. These medications may help the patient control urges to binge or purge. Studies show, however, that therapy directed at changing bulimics' behaviors is generally more successful than drug therapy.

Researchers are still working to understand bulimia and to track the recovery rates of patients. The data available on recovery reflect only patients who have sought treatment for their eating disorder. That is, people who binge and purge but never get treatment are not reflected in statistics that estimate recovery rates.

For those who do seek treatment, about 50 to 70 percent are able to overcome bulimia for periods of about six months to six years. However, an estimated 30 to 50 percent of treated people return to bulimic behaviors during this interval.[3]

In the long run—say, at about ten years after diagnosis—about 70 percent of patients have no clinical eating disorder. About 20 percent continue to practice some bulimic behaviors, though their condition is not severe enough to warrant a clinical diagnosis. Their condition is called a subthreshold eating disorder. About 10 percent of diagnosed patients have returned to a full-blown case of the disorder. In the ten-year population, less than 1 percent of cases of bulimia nervosa result in death.[4]

The powerful urge to consume huge quantities of food at one sitting can be frustrating, frightening, or infuriating.

9
BINGE EATING DISORDER

Binge eating is a disorder characterized by frequent episodes of consuming especially large amounts of food. While this aspect of the disorder is like bulimia nervosa, the binge eater does not purge the food or engage in physical activities to compensate for gorging. On average, the episodes of binge eating occur at least two days a week for six months. The binge episode may occur in a single sitting, such as during a two-hour period in which the binger consumes several thousand calories. Such gorging does not always occur in distinct episodes. The eating may take place throughout the day as several large meals or as continuous "grazing." Most people with binge eating disorder are overweight or obese.

Binge eating was not identified as an eating disorder until the early 1990s. While obesity was understood to carry health risks, binge eating had not been recognized as a medical disorder that, just as anorexia and bulimia, requires specialized treatment. Research into binge eating disorder is not yet as extensive as research into other eating disorders. Initial findings, however, suggest that the disorder may begin in early childhood. Despite the possibility of such early onset, patients with the disorder are typically older, in the forty-six- to fifty-five-year-old range, according to the National Institutes of

Health. The disorder afflicts three females for every two males.[2] Overall, approximately 2 to 3 percent of both adolescents and adults suffer from binge eating disorder.[3]

Someone who occasionally overeats or "pigs out" is not classified as a binge eater. Binge eating, like anorexia and bulimia, is an eating disorder that requires medical and psychological treatment. The following list gives some of the behaviors and feelings associated with this disorder.

SOME SYMPTOMS OF BINGE EATING DISORDER

- Repeated episodes of binge eating—usually two days a week or more for six months.
- A feeling of lack of control over eating or inability to stop eating.
- Eating much faster than normal during the binge, often too frenzied to taste the food.
- Eating huge quantities of food when not physically hungry.
- Eating alone to hide the amount of food being consumed.
- Feelings of guilt, shame, or disgust following the binge.
- Overweight or obesity.

MEDICAL CONSEQUENCES

People who suffer from binge eating disorder are at risk for health problems associated with obesity. The most common cause of death in the United States is coronary disease, and the occurrence of this disease is directly related to excess body fat and body weight. In fact, the American Heart Association cites obesity as a major risk factor for coronary heart disease.

Obese men and women also have a greater risk of stroke,

hyperglycemia, high blood pressure, high blood cholesterol, gallstones, gallbladder disease, and diabetes. Scientists also see higher rates of endometrial and gallbladder cancer among the overweight and obese than in the average population. As well, the occurrence of osteoarthritis of the knees and hips is associated with excessive body weight.

Researchers also report that obesity affects a person's quality of life. People with a high body mass index or high weight have reduced ability to be physically active. They are more likely to suffer physical pain and to have a diminished sense of well-being.

PSYCHOLOGICAL PATTERNS
OF BINGE EATERS

People with binge eating disorder typically gorge in private. The episodes of binging usually bring deep feelings of embarrassment or shame. Binge eaters feel bad enough about their compulsive binging sessions without having to deal with others' seeing what they are doing. Younger binge eaters may hide their behavior to avoid "getting in trouble" with a parent for consuming such large quantities of food. Older binge eaters may not want to explain to parents, either, or to roommates or spouses, what they are doing or to deal with the reactions of those close to them. Consequently, they binge alone and carefully dispose of the evidence.

People with binge eating disorder tend to have unrealistic or distorted ideas about their body weight and shape. In this regard, they are like people suffering from bulimia or anorexia. Their level of dissatisfaction with their bodies is about the same as that of bulimics. This is a higher level of dissatisfaction than that found in an average person who is obese but does not have an eating disorder.

Negative (low) self-esteem is common in binge eaters. The victim may have little skill in taking part in social situations.

Routine activities with friends, classmates, or other groups of people can seem overwhelming. These situations can plunge the binger into feelings of powerlessness, failure, depression, or anxiety. Like other people with eating disorders, binge eaters may try to sidestep social situations, especially those involving food.

Researchers see a connection between dieting and the onset (beginning) of binge eating patterns. About half of binge eaters who are obese say they first binged after attempts to diet. Other obese people with binge eating disorder say they began binging before or at about the same time as dieting for the first time. What do these connections suggest? Binge eating is one possible result of restricting food intake and interrupting healthy eating patterns. Dieting prevents the feeling of satiety that follows eating until comfortably full. Real hunger and the lack of satiety contribute to a binge eater's overpowering urge to gorge.

TREATMENT OF BINGE EATING DISORDER

The main goal of treatment for binge eating disorder is to teach patients how to eat in response to hunger, not in reaction to emotions such as depression, loneliness, or anxiety. Patients learn how to eat and to exercise in amounts that maintain appropriate weights for their heights. A nutritionist may work with patients to teach them how to choose a variety of healthful foods with an occasional treat of sweets or fast food. Regular, planned mealtimes and snacks help establish healthy eating behaviors. Eating only until hunger is sated is a crucial ability to develop. Parents of children or adolescents with binge eating disorder are encouraged to allow the kids to stop eating when comfortably full—regardless of whether they have cleaned their plates.

During treatment, patients with binge eating disorder are instructed about healthy portion and meal sizes. A patient may not know that one serving of meat is about the size of a deck of cards, not an entire 12-ounce steak. A serving of breakfast cereal may not completely fill the cereal bowl. A serving of cooked rice or pasta is about the size of a tennis ball. Patients learn how to serve themselves reasonably sized portions of all food types, including desserts, and to use a tool such as MyPyramid to recall the number of servings of each food group they need each day. In short, patients gain perspective on how much they are eating and how much they need to eat.

Another goal in the treatment of patients with binge eating disorder is achieving a healthy body weight. Patients receive education about the energy and calories in foods and are guided in how to eat healthfully for weight loss. Having regular meal and snack times is useful in helping patients regulate how much they eat. Moreover, eating at regular times conditions the body to anticipate when it is "time to eat." As a result, hunger pangs cue patients when to eat and subside when the appetite is sated.

As with any eating disorder, binge eating disorder is tied, to some degree, to how patients relate to their family members. How family members express themselves, how they handle stress, how they perceive body weight, and how they approach food and mealtimes are all significant in forming the patient's disorder. Consequently, a binge eater will likely benefit from family therapy. The therapist may devise ways in which the family can change behaviors, attitudes, or habits in order to help patients regain control of their eating and to remain successful at eating healthfully.

As with any eating disorder, there are no quick solutions to binge eating disorder. Professional treatment is extremely effective in helping patients to understand the disorder and to make necessary lifestyle changes.

Children suffering from eating disorders experience many of the same symptoms exhibited by teens and adults with eating disorders.

10
OTHER EATING DISORDERS

Anorexia nervosa, studied since the late nineteenth century, and bulimia nervosa, first described in 1979, are considered the two main eating disorders. Nevertheless, an estimated 20 to 61 percent of patients seeking treatment for eating disorders do not have anorexia or bulimia.[1] The other eating disorders, including binge eating disorder, are grouped together as eating disorders not otherwise specified, or EDNOS. When a patient seeks treatment for an eating disorder other than the main two, he or she may be diagnosed with EDNOS.

Like anorexia and bulimia, other eating disorders are medical conditions requiring professional treatment. This is so because, like the two main eating disorders, any EDNOS is an ongoing disruption to normal patterns of eating and eating-related behaviors. The disordered behavior focuses on controlling body weight and results in harm to the person's physical health and/or mental well being.

All eating disorders grouped as EDNOS meet the criteria for an eating disorder but not the criteria for either anorexia or bulimia. Some of these other disorders are binge eating disorder (discussed in chapter nine), childhood-onset eating disorders, and night-eating syndrome. EDNOS also includes subthreshold disorders, in which the patient exhibits most, but not all, of the criteria for anorexia or bulimia. As can be seen, EDNOS is a large group. This chapter gives information about eating disorders in this category.

CHILDHOOD-ONSET EATING DISORDERS

Usually, eating disorders first develop in teenagers or young adults. However, children age thirteen and under also develop eating disorders, although usually no earlier than age seven. In diagnosing these children, specialists call the condition a childhood-onset eating disorder. These disorders include anorexia, bulimia, food-avoidance emotional disorder, selective eating, and pervasive refusal syndrome.

Anorexia

The occurrence of anorexia in children is not as frequent as among teenagers. The disorder occurs in both girls and boys. In fact, about 20 to 25 percent of children diagnosed with anorexia are boys, compared with only about 5 to 10 percent of adult men diagnosed.[2]

Diagnosing anorexia in children is more difficult than in teenagers who have entered puberty. For example, children's bodies are still growing, but each child's rate of growth is unique. Slowed growth may not be readily attributed to an eating disorder, but instead to normal variance. Children under age fourteen commonly have not had the growth spurts that are associated with entering puberty. Prepubescent girls have not begun to menstruate, so amenorrhea (the stopping of regular menstruation) is not a possible criterion for diagnosis.

Diagnosing anorexia in children depends on the presence of specific symptoms that are evident in children. These symptoms include many that were mentioned in chapter seven: weight loss or halted growth, food refusal, obsession with food and calories, phobic fear of being fat, malnutrition, excessive exercise, forced vomiting, and misuse of laxatives. The child may grow downy hair on the face and arms, have low blood pressure, have a slow heart rate, and have cold arms and legs due to poor blood circulation. Bones may lose density or stop growing.

Children with anorexia often are perfectionists and diligent workers in school. They commonly suffer from depression and anxiety. They often try to hide evidence of the disorder by making excuses for why they are not eating, or hiding food they supposedly ate. Girls may insist they are on a diet, while boys may claim they are trying to get fit. Both boys and girls may exercise compulsively. If an adult limits their running or biking, for example, they may exercise secretly in their rooms by doing hundreds of push-ups. Some children may misuse laxatives or force themselves to vomit after eating, but these practices are less common at this age.

About 50 to 66 percent of children with childhood-onset anorexia recover. The remainder continue to suffer physical and psychological difficulties related to the disorder, including delayed growth, osteoporosis, and impaired fertility.[3]

Bulimia

Childhood-onset bulimia is not as common as other eating disorders in childhood. Those children who do develop this disorder exhibit the same symptoms as older sufferers. Usually these children's ages fall at the older end of the seven-to-thirteen-year-old age range.

Food-avoidance emotional disorder

This eating disorder is found only in children. In many ways it resembles anorexia. The child severely restricts food intake and may suffer from depression. Weight loss—or the failure to gain necessary weight for normal growth—is as severe as, or more severe than, that seen in anorexic children. Other symptoms include phobias (irrational fears), obsessive behaviors (behavior caused by compulsive urges), and refusal to attend school. Unlike anorexic children, however, children with food-avoidance emotional disorder do not have a fear of gaining weight, and they do not have a distorted body image.

Selective eating

Children who suffer from this condition are very selective, or picky, about what they eat. For example, a child may choose four or five foods that he or she will eat and absolutely refuse to eat any other foods. Typical food choices in children with selective eating disorder are high in carbohydrates. As a result, the children usually do not lose weight or have problems with energy. These children have little or no concern about their body weight or size. The condition seems to afflict boys more than it does girls; however, researchers are not yet sure how many children, on average, have the condition.

Pervasive refusal syndrome

Children with pervasive refusal syndrome reject not only food but also refuse to drink, walk, talk, or take care of themselves in any way. If adults try to care for them in any way, say by offering food, such children react with terror or anger. Typically, children with pervasive refusal syndrome spend a great deal of time curled into a fetal position, moaning quietly. The exact cause, or causes, of the syndrome is unidentified, but the condition is life threatening.

Night-eating syndrome

First described in 1955, this eating disorder is character-ized by a lack of hunger during most of the day, followed by insomnia and great hunger during the night. People with this syndrome consume over half of their daily calories between about 8:00 pm and 6:00 am. The symptoms of insomnia and night hunger tend to be greater during times of stress. For some, the urge to eat during the night is weaker when stress in life lessens.

Approximately 1.5 percent of the general population suf-fers from this syndrome, but the percentage is higher among obese people. Among those who enroll in clinics for the obese, about 10 percent suffer from night-eating syndrome. About 25 percent of people who undergo surgery for their obesity suffer from night-eating syndrome.

Night-eating syndrome is not only about stress and night-time eating. Sufferers also have a sleep disorder and a mood disorder. They have trouble falling asleep at night, and, even then, they wake up two or three times during the night. Each time they wake up, they eat a snack or small meal averaging about 270 calories. These foods tend to be high in carbohy-drates and low in protein. The urge to eat carbohydrate-rich foods may result from the fact that carbohydrates "e-mail" the brain to produce more serotonin. Serotonin induces sleep. Moreover, in people who do not have night-eating syndrome, levels of the hormone leptin rise at night, shutting down the appetite. In night eaters, however, leptin levels tend not to rise. These people's appetites, therefore, continue at full strength throughout the night. If you have ever awakened to a hungry, growling stomach, you may have some idea of what this syndrome is like.

SPECIAL CIRCUMSTANCES
AND EATING DISORDERS

Most eating disorders first appear in people in their teens or twenties. This is a time in young people's lives when they tend to be active in sports. Those in their twenties often are starting families. When it comes to eating disorders, athletes and pregnant women have particular risks.

Sports

Sports alone do not cause eating disorders. An athlete striving to reach his or her peak physical form, however, may be especially vulnerable to developing an eating disorder. For one thing, the sport itself may encourage having particularly lean bodies, as in ballet, gymnastics, cross country, and track and field events. Wrestlers may struggle to stay under a given weight to compete in a desired weight class. For many athletes, extensive training combined with special diets can result in low body weight. In addition, it is commonly assumed that an athlete can never train too much or too hard. Athletes are urged to "go for the burn" to build skill, strength, or speed. Teammates, coaches, or peers may tease an athlete for "wimping out" if he or she cannot

Athletes often must deal with unrealistic expectations for body shape or size.

keep up with the training schedule, rain or shine, good health or poor health.

A continued focus on shedding body weight and keeping it off can lead to anorexia or bulimia. Women may stop having their periods due to a low body mass index. Men may experience a drop in testosterone levels and loss of sexual desire. Both women and men athletes with anorexia or bulimia experience the symptoms of these disorders, described in chapters seven and eight. Over time, an athlete with an eating disorder experiences a decline in athletic ability and performance. Prolonged exercise coupled with an eating disorder can lead to kidney failure, heart attack, or death.

Pregnancy

Many women in their twenties start to think about starting families. This is a time when pregnancy, both planned and unplanned, is common. Teenage girls, too, may become pregnant. Unfortunately, the teens and twenties are also the years when most eating disorders develop. A woman with an eating disorder may have trouble conceiving a child. For example, an anorexic woman who does not have her periods cannot get pregnant. With other eating disorders, women may be incapable of carrying the baby to term. The result may be a miscarriage, a stillbirth, or a premature birth.

A healthy pregnancy means gaining weight at a steady rate. The American Pregnancy Association recommends that a woman of healthy weight who becomes pregnant should gain about 25 to 35 pounds during her pregnancy. An underweight woman is encouraged to gain more, about 28 to 40 pounds. An overweight woman is advised to gain less, about 15 to 25 pounds.[4] A woman who has a fear of gaining weight and being fat may be devastated to find out she is pregnant. Her emotional problems may intensify; she may have urges to harm herself or end the pregnancy. Obese women who become pregnant experience increased health risks. In some cases, however, a woman with an eating disorder sees pregnancy as a time to let go of her weight concerns and use the pregnancy as an excuse to take a break from food restriction.

For any woman, pregnancy is a time when nutrition takes on heightened importance, for she is eating to meet her own nutritional needs plus those of her unborn baby. Babies born to women with eating disorders have increased physical and emotional problems, and they are more likely to be smaller, weaker, and slower to grow than other babies. As they get older, these children may lag behind developmentally and emotionally. Developing social skills and relationships with other people may be more challenging for them. Researchers are not completely sure whether these developmental problems result from the mother's eating disorder during pregnancy or from being raised by a woman with an eating disorder and the related emotional problems.

RECOVERY AND EDNOS

Researchers do not yet fully understand the course and outcome of eating disorders classified as EDNOS, although they have made some discoveries. One study looked at people with subthreshold anorexia or bulimia (in other words, they did not have full-blown cases of the disorders). After about three-and-a-half years, almost half of the participants in the study had developed clinical anorexia or bulimia, while only a few had recovered.[5] Other studies have looked at binge eating disorder, finding that it rarely develops into another eating disorder.[6] Besides that, periods of remission seem to be common with this disorder, with or without treatment. The course and recovery rates of other EDNOS are poorly understood at this time.

PREVENTING EATING DISORDERS

Most of the research on preventing eating disorders has been done since 1990. In other words, prevention of eating disorders is a relatively new field of research. Specialists in the field, however, have produced some useful findings. In her article "Prevention of Eating Disorders," Niva Piran of the Department of Applied Psychology at the Ontario Institute for Studies in Education writes:

> The one factor that has consistently emerged from these studies as predicting the future development of eating disorders is weight concerns and the presence of eating disorder symptoms.[7]

To prevent an eating disorder, or to recognize the early signs of one that may be developing, knowledge about the subject is crucial. Reading the information in this book is a good place to start your education about eating disorders, risk factors, and warning signs. The Web sites and Further Reading suggestions at the back of this book are great sources of additional information.

Besides learning facts about eating disorders, perhaps the best thing you can do for yourself is to safeguard your physical health by eating and exercising wisely, and to assess and nurture your emotional health, including your self-esteem and body image. Putting your knowledge into practice will help you thrive both physically and mentally. You can use the information in this book as a starting point, but don't hesitate to seek help from parents, friends, teachers, counselors, or doctors as needed.

APPENDIXES

Appendix A

CDC Growth Charts: United States

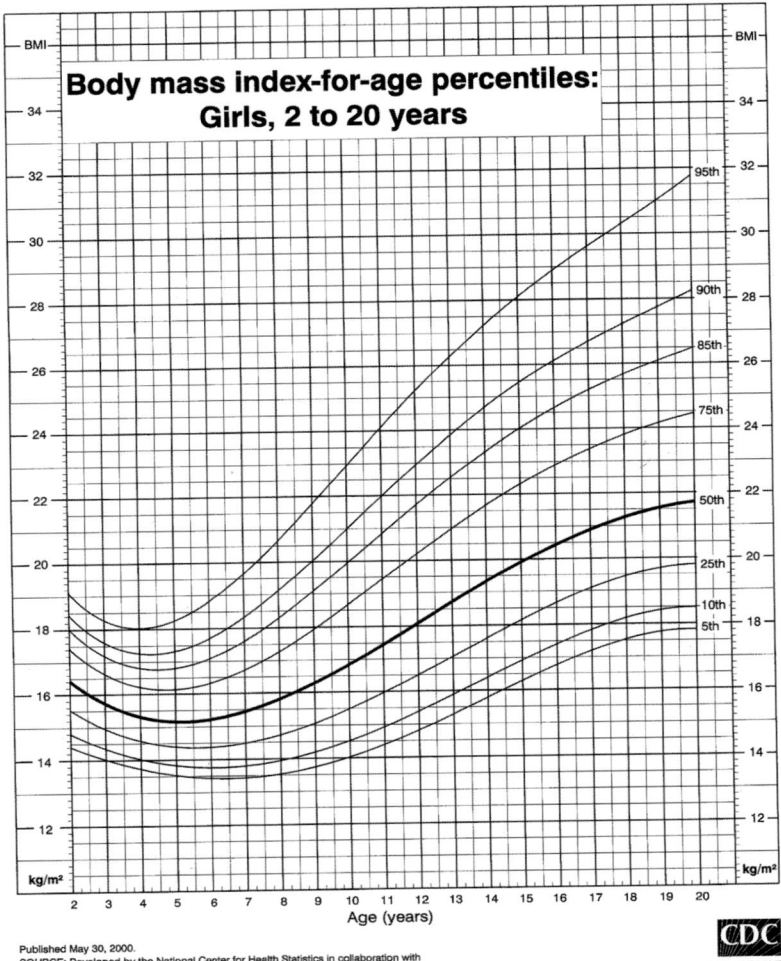

Body mass index-for-age percentiles: Girls, 2 to 20 years

Published May 30, 2000.
SOURCE: Developed by the National Center for Health Statistics in collaboration with the National Center for Chronic Disease Prevention and Health Promotion (2000).

CDC
SAFER · HEALTHIER · PEOPLE™

A BMI-for-age less than the 5th percentile indicates underweight. A BMI between the 5th and 84th percentiles indicates a normal weight. A BMI between the 85th and 94th percentiles indicates a risk of overweight, and a BMI greater than or equal to the 95th percentile indicates overweight.

Appendix B

CDC Growth Charts: United States

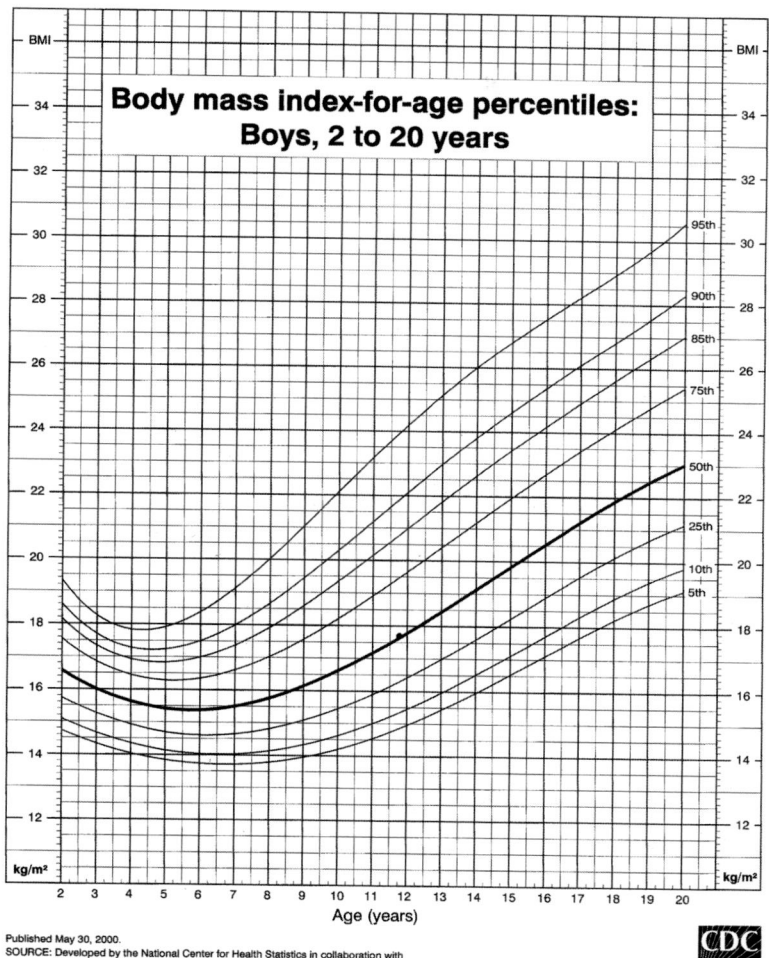

Body mass index-for-age percentiles: Boys, 2 to 20 years

Published May 30, 2000.
SOURCE: Developed by the National Center for Health Statistics in collaboration with the National Center for Chronic Disease Prevention and Health Promotion (2000).

CDC
SAFER · HEALTHIER · PEOPLE™

A BMI-for-age less than the 5th percentile indicates underweight. A BMI between the 5th and 84th percentiles indicates a normal weight. A BMI between the 85th and 94th percentiles indicates a risk of overweight, and a BMI greater than or equal to the 95th percentile indicates overweight .

Appendix C

Dietary Reference Intakes (DRIs): Recommended Intakes for Individuals, Total Water and Macronutrients
Food and Nutrition Board, Institute of Medicine, National Academies

Life Stage Group	Total Water[a] (L/d)	Carbo-hydrate (g/d)	Total Fiber (g/d)	Fat (g/d)	Linoleic Acid (g/d)	a-Linolenic Acid (g/d)	Protein (g/d)
Infants							
0-6 mo	0.7*	60*	ND	31*	4.4*	0.5*	9.1*
7-12 mo	0.8*	95*	ND	30*	4.6*	0.5*	11.0+
Children							
1-3 y	1.3*	130	19*	ND	7*	0.7*	13
4-8 y	1.7*	130	25*	ND	10*	0.9*	19
Males							
9-13 y	2.4*	130	31*	ND	12*	1.2*	34
14-18 y	3.3*	130	38*	ND	16*	1.6*	52
19-30 y	3.7*	130	38*	ND	17*	1.6*	56
31-50 y	3.7*	130	38*	ND	17*	1.6*	56
51-70 y	3.7*	130	30*	ND	14*	1.6*	56
>70 y	3.7*	130	30*	ND	14*	1.6*	56
Females							
9-13 y	2.1*	130	26*	ND	10*	1.0*	34
14-18 y	2.3*	130	26*	ND	11*	1.1*	46
19-30 y	2.7*	130	25*	ND	12*	1.1*	46
31-50 y	2.7*	130	25*	ND	12*	1.1*	46
51-70 y	2.7*	130	21*	ND	11*	1.1*	46
>70 y	2.7*	130	21*	ND	11*	1.1*	46
Pregnancy							
14-18 y	3.0*	175	28*	ND	13*	1.4*	71
19-30 y	3.0*	175	28*	ND	13*	1.4*	71
31-50 y	3.0*	175	28*	ND	13*	1.4*	71
Lactation							
14-18 y	3.8*	210	29*	ND	13*	1.3*	71
19-30 y	3.8*	210	29*	ND	13*	1.3*	71
31-50 y	3.8*	210	29*	ND	13*	1.3*	71

NOTE: This table represents Recommended Dietary Allowances (RDAs) in bold type and Adequate Intakes (AIs) in ordinary type followed by an asterisk (*). RDAs and AIs may both be used as goals for individual intake. RDAs are set to meet the needs of almost all (97 to 98 percent) individuals in a group. For healthy breastfed infants, the AI is the mean intake. The AI for other life stage and gender groups is believed to cover the needs of all individuals in the group, but lack of data or uncertainty in the data prevent being able to specify with confidence the percentage of individuals covered by this intake. The plus (+) symbol indicates a change from the prepublication copy due to a calculation error.
a Total water includes all water contained in food, beverages, and drinking water.
b Based on g protein per kg of body weight for the reference body weight, e.g., for adults 0.8 /kg body weight for the reference body weight.
c Not determined.
SOURCES: *Dietary Reference Intakes for Energy, Carbohydrate, Fiber, Fat, Fatty Acids, Cholesterol, Protein, and Amino Acids (2002/2005); Dietary Reference Intakes for Water, Potassium, Sodium, Chloride, and Sulfate (2005).* These reports may be accessed via http///www.nap.edu.

Appendix D

Reference Intakes (DRIs): Acceptable Macronutrient Distribution Ranges Food and Nutrition Board, Institute of Medicine, National Academies

Macronutrient	Range (percent of energy)		
	Children, 1-3 y	Children, 4-18 y	Adults
Fat	30-40	25-35	20-35
n -6 Polyunsaturated fatty acids[a] (linoleic acid)	5-10	5-10	5-10
n -3 Polyunsaturated fatty acids[a] (linolenic acid)	0.6-1.2	0.6-1.2	0.6-1.2
Carbohydrate	45-65	45-65	45-65
Protein	5-20	10-30	10-35

[a] Approximately 10 percent of the total can come from loner-chain n-3 or n-6 fatty acids.

SOURCE: *Dietary Reference Intakes for Energy, Carbohydrate, Fiber, Fat, Fatty Acids, Cholesterol, Protein, and Amino Acids* (2002/2005).

Appendix E

Dietary Reference Intakes: Recommended Intakes for Individuals: Vitamins

Life Stage Group	Vitamin A (µg/day)[a]	Vitamin C (mg/day)	Vitamin D (µg/day)[b,c]	Vitamin E (mg/day)[d]	Vitamin K (µg/day)	Thiamin (mg/day)	Riboflavin (mg/day)	Niacin (mg/day)[e]	Vitamin B₆ (mg/day)	Folate (µg/day)[f]	Vitamin B₁₂ (µg/day)	Pantothenic Acid (mg/day)	Biotin (µg/day)	Choline[g] (mg/day)
Infants														
0-6 mo	400*	40*	5*	4*	2.0*	0.2*	0.3*	2*	0.1*	65*	0.4*	1.7*	5*	125*
7-12 mo	500*	50*	5*	5*	2.5*	0.3*	0.4*	4*	0.3*	80*	0.5*	1.8*	6*	150*
Children														
1-3 y	300	15	5*	6	30*	0.5	0.5	6	0.5	150	0.9	2*	8*	200*
4-8 y	400	25	5*	7	55*	0.6	0.6	8	0.5	200	1.2	3*	12*	250*
Males														
9-13 y	600	45	5*	11	60*	0.9	0.9	12	1.0	300	1.8	4*	20*	315*
14-18 y	900	75	5*	15	75*	1.2	1.3	16	1.3	400	2.4	5*	25*	550*
19-30 y	900	90	5*	15	120*	1.2	1.3	16	1.3	400	2.4	5*	30*	550*
31-50 y	900	90	5*	15	120*	1.2	1.3	16	1.3	400	2.4	5*	30*	550*
51-70 y	900	90	10*	15	120*	1.2	1.3	16	1.7	400	2.4[h]	5*	30*	550*
>70 y	900	90	15*	15	120*	1.2	1.3	16	1.7	400	2.4[h]	5*	30*	550*
Females														
9-13 y	600	45	5*	11	60*	0.9	0.9	12	1.0	300	1.8	4*	20*	375*
14-18 y	700	65	5*	15	75*	1.0	1.0	14	1.2	400[i]	2.4	5*	25*	400*
19-30 y	700	75	5*	15	90*	1.1	1.1	14	1.3	400[i]	2.4	5*	30*	425*
31-50 y	700	75	5*	15	90*	1.1	1.1	14	1.3	400[i]	2.4	5*	30*	425*
51-70 y	700	75	10*	15	90*	1.1	1.1	14	1.5	400	2.4[h]	5*	30*	425*
>70 y	700	75	15*	15	90*	1.1	1.1	14	1.5	400	2.4[h]	5*	30*	425*
Pregnancy														
≤18 y	750	80	5*	15	75*	1.4	1.4	18	1.9	600[j]	2.6	6*	30*	450*
14-18 y	770	85	5*	15	90*	1.4	1.4	18	1.9	600[j]	2.6	6*	30*	450*
19-30 y	770	85	5*	15	90*	1.4	1.4	18	1.9	600[j]	2.6	6*	30*	450*
Lactation														
≤18 y	1200	115	5*	19	75*	1.4	1.6	17	2.0	500	2.8	7*	35*	550*
14-18 y	1300	120	5*	19	90*	1.4	1.6	17	2.0	500	2.8	7*	35*	550*
19-30 y	1300	120	5*	19	90*	1.4	1.6	17	2.0	500	2.8	7*	35*	550*

NOTE: This table (taken from the DRI reports, see www.nap.edu) presents Recommended Dietary Allowances (RDAs) in **bold** type and Adequate Intakes (AIs) in ordinary type followed by an asterisk (*). RDAs and AIs may both be used as goals for individual intakes. RDAs are set up to meet the needs of almost all (97–98%) individuals in a group. For healthy breastfed infants, the AI is the mean intake. The AI for all other life stage and gender groups is believed to cover needs of all individuals in the group, but lack of data or uncertainty in the data prevent being able to specify with confidence the percentage of individuals covered by this intake.

[a]As retinol activity equivalents (RAEs). 1 RAE = 1 µg retinol, 12 µg β-carotene, 24 µg β-carotene, or 24 µg β-cryptoxanthin in foods. To calculate RAEs from REs of provitamin A carotenoids in foods, divide RE by 2. For preformed vitamin A in foods or supplements and for provitamin A carotenoids in supplements, 1 RE = 1 RAE.

[b]Cholecalciferol. 1 µg cholecalciferol = 40 IU vitamin D.

[c]In the absence of exposure to adequate sunlight.

[d]As α-tocopherol, which includes RRR-α-tocopherol, the only form of α-tocopherol that occurs naturally in foods, and the 2R-stereoisomeric forms of α-tocopherol (RRR-, RSR-, RRS-, and RSS-α-tocopherol). Does not include the 2S-stereoisomeric forms of α-tocopherol (SRR-, SSR-, SRS-, and SSS- α -tocopherol), also found in food and supplements.

[e]As niacin equivalents (NEs), 1mg niacin = 60 mg tryptophan; 0-6 months = preformed niacin (not NE).

[f]As dietary folate equivalents (DFEs). 1 DFE = 1 µg food folate = 0.6 µg folic acid from fortified food or as a supplement consumed with food = 0.5 µg of a supplement taken on an empty stomach.

[g]Although AIs have been set for choline, there are few data to assess whether a dietary supplement of choline is needed at all stages of the life cycle, and it may be that the choline requirement can be met by endogenous synthesis at some of these stages.

[h]Because 10-30% of older people may malabsorb food-bound B₁₂, it is advisable for those older than 50 years to meet their RFD mainly by consuming foods fortified with B₁₂ or containing B₁₂.

[i]In view of evidence linking folate intake with neural tube defects in the fetus, it is recommended that all women capable of becoming pregnant consume 400 µg from supplements or fortified foods in addition to intake of food folate from a varied diet.

[j]It is assumed that women will consume 400 µg from supplements or fortified foods until their pregnancy is confirmed and they enter prenatal care, which ordinarily occurs after the end of the periconceptional period – the critical time for neural tube formation.

Appendix F

Dietary Reference Intakes: Recommended Intakes for Individuals: Minerals

Life Stage Group	Calcium (mg/day)	Chromium (µg/day)	Copper (µg/day)	Fluoride (mg/day)	Iodine (µg/day)	Iron (mg/day)	Magnesium (mg/day)	Manganese (mg/day)	Molybdenum (µg/day)	Phosphorus (mg/day)	Selenium (µg/day)	Zinc (mg/day)
Infants												
0-6 mo	210*	0.2*	200*	0.01*	110*	0.27*	30*	0.003*	2*	100*	15*	2*
7-12 mo	270*	5.5*	220*	0.5*	130*	11	75*	0.6*	3*	275*	20*	3
Children												
1-3 y	500*	11*	340	0.7*	90	7	80	1.2*	17	460	20	3
4-8 y	800*	15*	440	1*	90	10	130	1.5*	22	500	30	5
Males												
9-13 y	1,300*	25*	700	2*	120	8	240	1.9*	34	1,250	40	8
14-18 y	1,300*	35*	890	3*	150	11	410	2.2*	43	1,250	55	11
19-30 y	1,000*	35*	900	4*	150	8	400	2.3*	45	700	55	11
31-50 y	1,000*	35*	900	4*	150	8	420	2.3*	45	700	55	11
51-70 y	1,200*	30*	900	4*	150	8	420	2.3*	45	700	55	11
>70 y	1,200*	30*	900	4*	150	8	420	2.3*	45	700	55	11
Females												
9-13 y	1,300*	21*	700	2*	120	8	240	1.6*	34	1,250	40	8
14-18 y	1,300*	24*	890	3*	150	15	360	1.6*	43	1,250	55	9
19-30 y	1,000*	25*	900	3*	150	18	310	1.8*	45	700	55	8
31-50 y	1,000*	25*	900	3*	150	18	320	1.8*	45	700	55	8
51-70 y	1,200*	20*	900	3*	150	8	320	1.8*	45	700	55	8
>70 y	1,200*	20*	900	3*	150	8	320	1.8*	45	700	55	8
Pregnancy												
≤18 y	1,300*	29*	1,000	3*	220	27	400	2.0*	50	1,250	60	13
14-18 y	1,000*	30*	1,000	3*	220	27	350	2.0*	50	1,250	60	13
19-30 y	1,000*	30*	1,000	3*	220	27	360	2.0*	50	700	60	11
Lactation												
≤18 y	1,300*	44*	1,300	3*	290	10	360	2.6*	50	1,250	70	14
14-18 y	1,300*	45*	1,300	3*	290	9	310	2.6*	50	700	70	12
19-30 y	1,300*	45*	1,300	3*	290	9	320	2.6*	50	700	70	12

NOTE: This table (taken from the DRI reports, see www.nap.edu) presents Recommended Dietary Allowances (RDAs) in **bold** type and Adequate Intakes (AIs) in ordinary type followed by an asterisk (*). RDAs and AIs may both be used as goals for individual intakes. RDAs are set up to meet the needs of almost all (97-98%) individuals in a group. For healthy breastfed infants, the AI is the mean intake. The AI for all other life stage and gender groups is believed to cover needs of all individuals in the group, but lack of data or uncertainty in the data prevents being able to specify with confidence the percentage of individuals covered by this intake.

Metric Conversion Chart

You can use the chart below to convert from U.S. measurements to the metric system.

Weight
1 ounce = 28 grams
1/2 pound (8) ounces = 227 grams

1 pound = .45 kilogram
2.2 pounds = 1 kilogram

Liquid Volume
1 teaspoon = 5 milliliters
1 tablespoon = 15 milliliters
1 fluid ounce = 30 milliliters
1 cup = 240 milliliters
1 pint = 480 milliliters
1 quart = .95 liter

Length
1/4 inch = .6 centimeter
1/2 inch = 1.25 centimeters

1 inch = 2.5 centimeters

Temperature
100°F = 40°C
110°F = 45°C
350°F = 180°C
375°F = 190°C
400°F = 200°C
425°F = 220°C
450°F = 235°C

Body Mass Index Conversion Formula (Metric)

$$BMI= \left(\frac{\text{weight in kilograms}}{(\text{height in meters}) \times (\text{height in meters})} \right) \times 703$$

notes

Introduction
1. Fairburn and Walsh, 171.

Chapter 1
1. National Eating Disorders Association. "General Information: Facts for Activists (or Anyone!)."
2. Ogden, Cynthia L. et al. "Mean Body Weight, Height, and Body Mass Index, United States 1960—2002."

Chapter 2
1. Anorexia Nervosa and Related Eating Disorders.

Chapter 4
1. Dietz, William H., and Loraine Stern, eds., 145.
2. National Eating Disorders Association. "General Information: Facts for Activists (or Anyone!)."

Chapter 5
1. Prouty, Anne M. "College Women: Eating Behaviors and Help-Seeking Preferences."
2. Brown, Jane D., and Elizabeth M. Witherspoon. "The Mass Media and American Adolescents' Health," 158, 159.
3. Boutelle, Kerri et al. "Weight Control Behaviors Among Obese, Overweight, and Nonoverweight Adolescents," 532.
4. Paxton, Raheem J., Robert F. Valois, and J. Wanzer Drane. "Correlates of Body Mass Index, Weight Goals, and Weight-Management Practices Among Adolescents," 136, Hill, James O. et al. "Obesity and the Environment: Where Do We Go from Here?" 853.

Chapter 6
1. Boutelle, Kerri et al., p. 532.

2. Paxton, Valois, and Drane, 136, and Hill, James O. et al. "Obesity and the Environment: Where Do We Go from Here?" 853.

3. Centers for Disease Control and Prevention. "Overweight and Obesity: Obesity Trends: U.S. Obesity Trends 1985—2004."

4. Sylvester, Gina Pazzaglia, Cheryl Achterberg, and Jerome Williams. "Children's Television and Nutrition: Friends or Foes," 8, 9.

5. Ibid., 6.

6. Andersen, Ross E. et al. "Relationship of Physical Activity and Television Watching with Body Weight and Level of Fatness Among Children," 940.

Chapter 7

1. Nemours Foundation. "Eating Disorders: Anorexia and Bulimia."

2. Dietz and Stern, 148.

3. Brown and Witherspoon, 159.

4. Ibid.

5. Nemours Foundation.

6. Dietz and Stern, 149.

7. Smolin, Lori A., and Mary B. Grosvenor. *Nutrition and Eating Disorders*, 91-92.

Chapter 8

1. Sullivan, Patrick F. "Course and Outcome of Anorexia Nervosa and Bulimia Nervosa," 227.

2. Smolin and Grosvenor, 94.

3. Ibid., 103.

4. Sullivan, 227.

Chapter 9

1. Grilo, Carlos M. "Binge Eating Disorder," 180.
2. National Institutes of Health, U.S. Department of Health and Human Services. "Binge Eating Disorder."
3. Grilo, 180.

Chapter 10

1. Fairburn and Walsh, 174.
2. Bryant-Waugh, Rachel, and Bryan Lask. "Childhood-Onset Eating Disorders," 211.
3. Bryant-Waugh and Lask, 212.
4. American Pregnancy Association. "Eating for Two."
5. Fairburn and Walsh, 175.
6. Ibid.
7. Piran, Niva. "Prevention of Eating Disorders," 368.

amenorrhea: The absence or cessation of menstruation in a female.

anorexia nervosa: An eating disorder characterized by a weight 15 percent below normal for age and height, an intense fear of gaining weight/being fat, and distorted body-image. In females, another characteristic is amenorrhea.

antioxidants: Vitamins that protect against damage and destruction of cells in the body.

appetite: An urge to eat; it may or may not be related to actual hunger.

binge: To eat unusually large amounts of food in one sitting.

binge eating disorder: An eating disorder characterized by repeated episodes of eating large amounts of food. People with this disorder do not engage in purging behaviors.

body image: How you feel "in your own skin," how you think others see you, and how you think you measure up to physical standards set by yourself and others.

body mass index (BMI): A measurement of body fat in relation to body height. A healthy BMI falls in the range of 18.5—24.9.

bulimia nervosa: An eating disorder characterized by repeated episodes of eating large amounts of food, followed by induced vomiting, misuse of laxatives, or excessive exercising.

calorie: The amount of heat energy required to raise the temperature of 1 gram of water by 1 degree Celsius at 1 atmospheric pressure. The energy in food is measured in calories.

carbohydrates: Sugars, starches, and most fibers: one of the six classes of nutrients. Simple carbohydrates are naturally occurring sugars, such as fructose in fruit; they are a quick source of energy. Complex carbohydrates provide longer-lasting energy and are found in most grain products, vegetables, and potatoes.

childhood-onset eating disorder: An eating disorder that manifests in someone between the ages of seven and thirteen. These disorders include anorexia, bulimia, food-avoidance emotional disorder, selective eating, and pervasive refusal syndrome.

diet: A pattern of eating, including the kinds of food and drink habitually consumed.

dietary reference intakes (DRIs): Recommended daily amounts of nutrients.

digestive process: The body's way of breaking down food to get nutrients and energy.

diuretic: Drugs to increase the amount of urine.

eating disorder: A pattern of eating intended to control weight and that is destructive to the person's physical and psychological health.

eating disorders not otherwise specified (EDNOS): A diagnostic category including all eating disorders except anorexia nervosa and bulimia nervosa.

food-avoidance emotional disorder: A childhood-onset eating disorder characterized by severe restriction of food but no fear of being fat and no distorted body image.

genetics: The hereditary makeup of a person; relating to or caused by genes.

kilocalorie: See calorie.

lipids: Fats: one of the six classes of nutrients.

minerals: Inorganic substances: one of the six classes of nutrients.

night-eating syndrome: An eating disorder characterized by a lack of hunger during most of the day, followed by insomnia, great hunger, and ravenous eating during the night.

nutrients: Substances needed by the body for energy and tissue building. The six classes of nutrients are carbohydrates, protein, lipids, vitamins, minerals, and water.

nutrition: The means by which a living organism takes in nourishment for energy, growth, and repair. Also, the science that studies the processes of organisms and food.

obese: Having a body mass index greater than thirty.

pervasive refusal syndrome: A childhood-onset eating disorder characterized by refusal to eat, drink, walk, talk, or take care of oneself in any way.

proteins: Chains of amino acids: one of the six classes of nutrients. Found in animal products such as eggs and meat, and certain vegetables, grains, and beans.

puberty: The period in life when a person's body changes from that of a child to that of an adult, normally capable of reproducing.

purge: To cause the body to get rid of food that was eaten, such as by forced vomiting or misuse of laxatives.

satiety: A feeling of fullness or satisfaction after eating.

selective eating: A childhood-onset eating disorder characterized by extreme pickiness in food choices. For example, a child may choose four or five foods that he will eat and absolutely refuse to eat any other foods.

self-image: How you see yourself; how you assess your personal qualities and individual worth.

set point: Regarding body weight, a term used to describe a weight that the body tends to maintain when a person eats healthfully when hungry, stops eating when full, and exercises moderately.

subthreshold eating disorder: A disordered pattern of eating that does not meet the full diagnostic criteria for a clinical eating disorder.

triglycerides: Fats in the diet, including saturated fats and unsaturated fats.

vitamins: Organic substances found in tiny amounts in plant and animal foods: one of the six classes of nutrients.

water: One of the six classes of nutrients. An adult's body is made up of 50 percent to 65 percent water.

wellness: Your state of physical and mental health.

FURTHER INFORMATION

Books

Bickerstaff, Linda. *Nutrition Sense: Counting Calories, Figuring Out Fats, and Eating Balanced Meals.* New York: Rosen Publishing Group, 2005.

Heaton, Jeanne Albronda, and Claudia J. Strauss. *Talking to Eating Disorders: Simple Ways to Support Someone with Anorexia, Bulimia, Binge Eating, or Body Image Issues.* New York: New American Library, 2005.

Heller, Tania. *Eating Disorders: A Handbook for Teens, Families, and Teachers.* Jefferson, NC: McFarland and Co., 2003.

Kittleson, Mark J., ed. *The Truth About Eating Disorders.* New York: Facts on File, 2004.

Kolodny, Nancy J. *The Beginner's Guide to Eating Disorders Recovery.* Carlsbad, CA: Gurze Books, 2004.

Lawton, Sandra Augustyn, editor. *Eating Disorders Information for Teens: Health Tips About Anorexia, Bulimia, Binge Eating, and Other Eating Disorders.* Detroit: Omnigraphics, 2005.

Silate, Jennifer. *Planning and Preparing Healthy Meals and Snacks: A Day-to-Day Guide to a Healthier Diet.* New York: Rosen Publishing Group, 2005.

Web Sites

The following Web sites are especially good locations for learning more about nutrition, eating disorders, and treatment.

Anorexia Nervosa and Related Eating Disorders, Inc.
http://www.anred.com
Information and resources on all eating disorders, not just

anorexia. Includes information on treatment, recovery, self-help, prevention strategies, statistics, and more.

Food and Nutrition Information Center
http://www.nal.usda.gov/fnic
Resources on food and nutrition for consumers, nutrition and health professionals, and educators. Click on "Topics A-Z" and then on "Adolescence" to find links to articles and Web sites especially for young people. Topics in this section include nutrition, body image, and fitness.

MyPyramid
http://www.mypyramid.gov
The USDA's Web site on the food guide pyramid. Includes an explanation of MyPyramid, dietary guidelines, tips for making healthful food choices, a special section for kids, and interactive tools to design your own healthy eating plan and to track your eating.

National Association of Anorexia Nervosa and Associated Disorders
http://www.anad.org
Information and resources on eating disorders, hotline counseling, support groups, referrals to health-care professionals, message board, chat rooms, and more.

National Eating Disorder Information Centre
http://www.nedic.ca
Includes questions and answers about eating disorders, suggestions for friends and families of people with eating disorders, recommended reading, a glossary, links to online resources, and more. Based in Toronto, Canada.

National Eating Disorders Association
http://www.nationaleatingdisorders.org
Click on the link at the top of the page to go to "Eating Disorders Info." You'll find a long list of links to pages that each focuses on one topic relating to eating disorders, including definitions, causes, prevention, body image, health, pregnancy, treatment, statistics, tips, and more.

Nemours Foundation: TeensHealth
http://www.kidshealth.org/teen
Teen-oriented information on everything from food and fitness to mental, physical, and sexual health. In the search box, type "eating disorders" to get a list of articles on eating disorders and related topics such as body image, fitness, weight, diets, malnutrition, therapy, helping friends, and more.

Something Fishy Website on Eating Disorders
http://www.somethingfishy.org
Includes articles about eating disorders, links to news stories, treatment information and links to treatment providers, online forums for sufferers and for families of sufferers, scheduled special-topic chats, and more.

NOTE: All Web Sites in this section were current as of January 1, 2007.

BIBLIOGRAPHY

American Pregnancy Association. "Eating for Two: Weight Influences on Pregnancy." http://www.american pregnancy.org/pregnancyhealth/eatingfortwo.html (12-12-05)

Andersen, Ross E. et al. "Relationship of Physical Activity and Television Watching with Body Weight and Level of Fatness Among Children." *JAMA*, vol. 279, no. 12 (March 25, 1998): 938-942.

Anorexia Nervosa and Related Eating Disorders, Inc. "Eating Disorder Warning Signs." http://www.anred.comwarn.html (12-5-05)

Boutelle, Kerri et al. "Weight Control Behaviors Among Obese, Overweight, and Nonoverweight Adolescents." *Journal of Pediatric Psychology*, vol. 27, no. 6 (2002): 531—540.

Brown, Jane D., and Elizabeth M. Witherspoon. "The Mass Media and American Adolescents' Health." Supplement article. *Journal of Adolescent Health*, vol. 31, no. 6S, (2002): 153—170.

Bryant-Waugh, Rachel, and Bryan Lask. "Childhood-Onset Eating Disorders." See Fairburn, Christopher G., and Kelly D. Brownell.

Centers for Disease Control and Prevention. "Overweight and Obesity: Obesity Trends: U.S. Obesity Trends 1985—2004." http://www.cdc.gov/nccdphp/dnpa/obesity/trend/maps (12-15-05)

Dietz, William H., and Loraine Stern, eds. *American Academy of Pediatrics Guide to Your Child's Nutrition.* New York: Villard, 1999.

Fairburn, Christopher G., and Kelly D. Brownell, eds. *Eating Disorders and Obesity: A Comprehensive Handbook.* 2nd ed. New York: Guilford Press, 2002.

Fairburn, Christopher G., and B. Timothy Walsh. "Atypical Eating Disorders (Eating Disorder Not Otherwise Specified)." See Fairburn, Christopher G., and Kelly D. Brownell.

Favor, Lesli J. *Everything You Need to Know About Growth Spurts and Delayed Growth.* New York: Rosen Publishing, 2002.

Food and Nutrition Board, Institute of Medicine of the National Academies. *Dietary Reference Intakes for Energy, Carbohydrate, Fiber, Fat, Fatty Acids, Cholesterol, Protein, and Amino Acids.* Washington, D.C.: National Academies Press, 2005.

Food and Nutrition Board, The National Academy of Sciences, "DRIs: Recommended Intakes for Individuals, Total Water and Macronutrients" and "DRIs: Estimated Average Requirements for Groups," 2005. http://www.nap.edu (4-20-06)

Grilo, Carlos M. "Binge Eating Disorder." See Fairburn, Christopher G., and Kelly D. Brownell.

Hensrud, Donald D., ed. *Mayo Clinic: Healthy Weight for Everybody.* Rochester, MN: Mayo Clinic Health Information, 2005.

Hensrud, Donald D., ed. *Mayo Clinic on Healthy Weight.* Rochester, MN: Kensington Publishing, 2000.

Hill, James O. et al. "Obesity and the Environment: Where Do We Go from Here?" *Science*, vol. 299 (2-7-03): 853—855.

National Center for Health Statistics in collaboration with the National Center for Chronic Disease Prevention and Health Promotion. "Body mass index-for-age percentiles: Boys, 2 to 20 years." http://www.cdc.gov/nchs/data/nhanes/ growthcharts/set2/chart%2015.pdf (3-27-06)

National Center for Health Statistics in collaboration with the National Center for Chronic Disease Prevention and Health Promotion. "Body mass index-for-age percentiles:

Girls, 2 to 20 years." http://www.cdc.gov/nchs/data/nhanes/ growthcharts/set2/chart%2016.pdf (3-27-06)

National Digestive Diseases Information Clearinghouse. "Your Digestive System and How It Works." http://digestive. nid-dk.nih.gov/ddiseases/pubs/yrdd (11-14-05)

National Eating Disorders Association. "General Information: Facts for Activists (or Anyone!)." http://www.nationaleatingdisorders.org/p.asp?WebPage_ID= 320&Profile_ID=95634 (11-22-05)

National Heart, Lung, and Blood Institute. "Body Mass Index Table." http://www.nhlbi.nih.gov/guidelines/obesity/ob_-home.htm (11-29-05)

Nemours Foundation. "Eating Disorders: Anorexia and Bulimia." http://www.kidshealth.org/teen/exercise/ problems/eat_-disorder.html (12-1-05)

Ogden, Cynthia L. et al. "Mean Body Weight, Height, and Body Mass Index, United States 1960-2002." Advance Data from Vital and Health Statistics 347 (10-27-04). http://www.cdc.gov/nchs/data/ad/ad347.pdf (11-09-05)

Paxton, Raheem J., Robert F. Valois, and J. Wanzer Drane. "Correlates of Body Mass Index, Weight Goals, and Weight-Management Practices Among Adolescents." *Journal of School Health*, vol. 74, no. 4 (2004): 136–143.

Piran, Niva. "Prevention of Eating Disorders." See Fairburn, Christopher G., and Kelly D. Brownell.

Prouty, Anne M. "College Women: Eating Behaviors and Help-Seeking Preferences." http://www.findarticles.com/ p/articles/mi_m2248/is_146_37/ai_89942836/print (12-13-05)

Smolin, Lori A., and Mary B. Grosvenor. *Nutrition and Eating Disorders*. Philadelphia: Chelsea House, 2005.

Sullivan, Patrick F. "Course and Outcome of Anorexia

Nervosa and Bulimia Nervosa." See Fairburn, Christopher G., and Kelly Brownell.

Sylvester, Gina Pazzaglia, Cheryl Achterberg, and Jerome Williams. "Children's Television and Nutrition: Friends or Foes?" *Nutrition Today,* vol. 30, no. 1, (1995): 6—15.

Tamborlane, William V., ed. *The Yale Guide to Children's Nutrition.* New Haven: Yale University Press, 1997.

United States Department of Agriculture, "MyPyramid: Food Intake Patterns," 2005. http://www.mypyramid.gov/downloads/MyPyramid_Food_Intake_Pattersn.pdf (4-17-06)

United States Department of Agriculture, "My-Pyramid: Mini Poster." http://www.mypyramid.gov/downloads/Mini-Poster.pdf (4-17-06)

United States Department of Health and Human Services, and United States Department of Agriculture. "Table 3: Estimated Calorie Requirements (in Kilocalories) for Each Gender and Age Group at Three Levels of Physical Activity." In Dietary Guidelines for Americans 2005. http://www.health-.gov/dietaryguidelines/dga2005/document/html/chapter2.htm#table3 (11-9-05)

INDEX

ABOUT THE AUTHOR

Lesli J. Favor has written eleven books on science, biography, and history topics for young people, including *Weighing In: Nutrition and Weight Management* in this series. She also has published numerous books and workbooks on grammar, writing, and test preparation in English Language Arts. She has a BA in English from the University of Texas at Arlington and an MA and PhD, both in English, from the University of North Texas. She lives in the Seattle area with her husband, son, two dogs, and horse.